NEWS/400
TECHNIC...
REFERENCE
SERIES

Bryan Meyers
series editor

Desktop
Guide to
Creating
CL
Commands

by Lynn Nelson

Library of Congress Cataloging-in-Publication Data

Nelson, Lynn, 1957-
    Desktop guide to creating CL commands / Lynn Nelson.
        p. cm. -- (News/400 technical reference series)
    Includes index.
    ISBN 1-882419-56-1. -- ISBN 1-882419-11-1
    1. IBM AS/400 (Computer)--Programming. I. Title. II. Series.
QA76.8.I25919N45 1996
002.2'45--dc20   96-10149
                                                                         CIP

Copyright © 1996 by DUKE PRESS
DUKE COMMUNICATIONS INTERNATIONAL
Loveland, Colorado

This book was printed and bound in the United States of America.

ISBN 1-882419-56-1

ISBN 1-882419-11-1 (*NEWS/400* Technical Reference Series)

1 2 3 4 5 6 KP 9 8 7 6

Table of Contents

Section 2: Command Tips and Techniques

Section 3: Advanced Topics

Section 4: Appendices

Introduction

The focus of this book is to build on your current understanding of command creation and whet your appetite for creating your own commands.

Programming on the IBM AS/400 offers you many choices. You can pick from various languages (e.g., RPG, COBOL), numerous utilities (e.g., SDA, RLU), different methods of using files (e.g., logical files, OPNQRYF) and many other special options (e.g., UIM panels, commands) to create a whole, functional, and robust application.

Many programmers, however, use the same methods over and over. For example, programmers often don't understand the true scope and power of command creation. But the capability to make new commands is extremely valuable in application programming. The focus of this book is to build on your current understanding of command creation and whet your appetite for creating your own commands.

User-Defined Commands

IBM's definition of commands is pretty terse:

A statement that requests a function of the system.

That description doesn't even begin to tell the story. By creating your own commands, you have a fast and powerful front end you can then use to invoke your own functions. This front-end interface includes automatic editing, parameter and message passing, sophisticated parameter dependencies, and online help. All this comes wrapped in a package of a system-supplied, automatic prompt screen.

Commands were originally the sole property of the programmers in IBM labs. They used commands to collect information from the users (us!) and then fed that information to system programs. Somewhere along the way, IBM decided to share the wealth with us. All programs, whether they are system programs or application programs, can now use this powerful technique.

Let's look at some commands we are all familiar with. Have you ever used WRKOUTQ (Work with Output Queue) or DSPOBJD (Display Object Description)? These are IBM-supplied commands. How about CRTCLPGM (Create CL Program) or DLTF (Delete File)? More IBM commands. IBM uses commands as the interface between the operating system and us, the users. Because IBM has given us the ability to create our own commands, we can use them for our application programs. These user-defined commands look and work exactly like IBM-supplied commands. And an unexpected bonus is that they are extremely easy to create.

Uses for Commands

You can use commands in application programming in many ways. The major uses this book covers are macro-like functions, user prompting, and selective prompting.

Macro-Like Functions

If you have used commands at all, the way you have used them has probably been in macro-like functions. Commands can provide functions that let you abbreviate frequently used tasks to a few simple keystrokes. For example, to automatically set up a frequently used library list, you can create a command that will save you the work of having to enter the library names every time you want to use a specific list. You can have different macro commands for different library lists to let you quickly move from one environment to another. You can create all kinds of operational commands that will customize your environment and save you keystrokes.

User Prompting

A more powerful use of commands, however, is in the area of user prompting. You can use a command to create an interactive prompt screen that calls a high-level language (HLL) program. The prompt screen you create with a command looks just like IBM's prompts and can perform editing, present lists of valid choices, display help, and provide many other features. For example, to let a user request a report, you can use a command to prompt for the required information, such as number of copies and the printer output queue. Commands can also prompt for parameters for application information — G/L numbers, range of department numbers, company, and division number.

Selective Prompting

Selective prompting lets you customize existing commands, either IBM-supplied or user-defined. You can determine which parameters to display or omit and which values to default, as well as pass variables to parameters. For example, if you want to let users work with spool files, you can use IBM's WRKSPLF (Work with Spool File) command with selective prompting to control which parameters are displayed and how they are defaulted. You will find this use of commands helpful in making operations easier. Also, by controlling what options are available, you can build a high level of control and security into your system.

Why Use Custom Commands?

You probably have managed to write many applications without ever once using your own commands. So you might be wondering why you should bother to learn how to create commands now. Or maybe you have played around with commands a little but have never really seen how they could help you in your applications. There are several reasons for learning how to use custom commands.

Commands provide a consistent user interface.

First, commands are an easy way to provide a quality and consistent user interface. The operative word here is consistent. Most users are already familiar with IBM's method of prompting; and your custom-defined commands will look and feel just like IBM's, right down to the function keys.

Commands are a snap to program. Creating a complex, powerful prompt screen is almost effortless; and your small investment of time will be returned many times over.

A final argument for creating custom commands for your applications is that IBM uses CL commands as the major interface between the operating system and users. If commands are flexible and powerful enough to provide the system functions that IBM needs, they should be more than adequate for some of your application programming requirements.

Getting Started

This book demonstrates how to use commands in application programming. The approach is functional, beginning with the most basic features and gradually building toward complex concepts. If you're just learning how to write commands, you'll want to start at the beginning and work through each chapter in order; if you have more experience, you can go straight to any chapter and find out what you need to know. Examples of source code illustrate each concept. At any point in your journey through this book, you can take what you have learned and create complete, usable commands. You will be delighted to see how quickly you can begin to incorporate new commands into your application programming. After you complete the book and become more experienced in creating commands, you can use the summary lists in the appendices as quick reference guides.

Section 1

Command Basics

Overview of Command Creation

Chapter 1

A command is an object, just like programs or files are objects. The command definition object is an object of type *CMD that you compile from a source member (type CMD) using the CRTCMD (Create Command) command. You create this source member via SEU or your favorite source editor.

The Command Processing Program

A command calls a command processing program (CPP) to perform its function.

A command only processes a request; it does not perform any application functions. The command calls a high-level language (HLL) or CL program to perform those functions. This called program is the command processing program (CPP). For example, suppose you have a program that prints your chart of accounts. By creating a command, you can have a prompt screen that asks users for a range of accounts they want printed. The command will create a prompt screen, edit the information users enter, even provide help text, and then pass the account range to the application program. The amount of effort required to create the command is minimal, and the results are impressive.

To create a command, you start with a command source member. Command source members are made up of command definition statements. The six statement types are

- CMD — Command
- PARM — Parameter
- ELEM — Element
- PMTCTL — Prompt Control
- QUAL — Qualifier
- DEP — Dependency

When using SEU to key a command into a source member, you may prompt (F4) any of the command definition statements for their keywords (the prompting will work only if the source member is type CMD).

The CRTCMD (Create Command) Command

CRTCMD compiles the command source member and names the CPP.

You use the CRTCMD command to compile the source member for the command into the command definition object. This command also names the program that will act as the CPP. This is an important point, because CRTCMD is the only place where the program that does the real work (the CPP) is ever referenced (see Figure 1.1). If you look only at the command source member, you never see a reference to the CPP. This lack of reference to the CPP confuses many novice command writers. Without the CPP, commands look like they are simply smoke and mirrors.

Figure 1.1 The CRTCMD Command

CRTCMD also defines optional command attributes, such as a validity checking program, a prompt-override program, and the help panel group (we will discuss these features in Section 3, Advanced Topics).

Figure 1.2 shows an example of the CRTCMD prompt screen for creating a command called TLL (Test Library List).

The first set of parameters, **Command** and **Library**, give the command its name and tell the system where to store the compiled object. The second set, **Program to process command** and its **Library**, define the program that this command will execute (the CPP) — in this case, the CL program TLLCL. The final three parameters, **Source file**, **Library**, and **Source member**, identify the source for the command. You'll notice that F10 is available to display more parameters, but we'll get into those later.

Figure 1.2 The CRTCMD Command Prompt Screen

```
                         Create Command (CRTCMD)

 Type choices, press Enter.

 Command . . . . . . . . . . . .    TLL_____     Name
   Library . . . . . . . . . . .      *CURLIB___  Name, *CURLIB
 Program to process command. . .    TLLCL_____    Name, *REXX
   Library . . . . . . . . . . .      *CURLIB___  Name, *LIBL, *CURLIB
 Source file . . . . . . . . . .    QCMDSRC___    Name
   Library . . . . . . . . . . .      *LIBL_____  Name, *LIBL, *CURLIB
 Source member . . . . . . . . .    *CMD_____    Name, *CMD




                                                                   Bottom
 F3=Exit   F4=Prompt   F5=Refresh   F10=Additional parameters  F12=Cancel
 F13=How to use this display       F24=More keys
```

Question: If CRTCMD is the command that creates a command, how was the CRTCMD command created? Is anyone else losing sleep over this? Presumably, the HLL program that is the CPP for the CRTCMD command was simply called directly, passing the appropriate parameters. After all, a command is just a front end to the program that performs the actual function.

The first section of this book will acquaint you with the command definition statements that make up the command source member. You can think of these statements as a sort of HLL in themselves — the language of commands. We'll begin with the first and most basic command definition statement, the CMD (Command) statement.

The CMD Statement

The CMD statement provides a title for the command.

The CMD statement is the only mandatory command definition statement. Its sole purpose is to provide the title text for the command prompt screen. You must specify CMD, however, even if the command is not used for prompting.

The CMD statement has one keyword, PROMPT. The following line of code is an example of a simple command macro, TLL (Test Library List), which executes the CL program TLLCL to change the library list. This command uses only the CMD statement.

```
CMD     PROMPT('Test Library List')
```

Remember that a command must have a CPP that does the work. The sample lines of code below represent the CL program that is the CPP for the command. What links the command above to this CL program is the CRTCMD process (already shown in Figure 1.2) that compiles the command.

```
PGM
CHGLIBL     LIBL(TESTLIB1 TESTLIB2 TESTLIB3 TESTLIB4)
ENDPGM
```

This sample macro command changes the library list for testing. The only difference between using the command (TLL) and using the CL program (TLLCL) is that the CL program must be called (CALL TLLCL), whereas the command is referenced directly (TLL). Using a command to create this type of macro simply saves a few keystrokes.

The real value of commands is in creating prompt screens.

The real value of commands is in creating prompt screens. The next example displays a prompt for the user to enter information required to run a report. This sample code shows a complete but simple command for prompting and illustrates how the CMD statement specifies the screen heading on the prompt screen.

```
CMD       PROMPT('Competitor Master File Listing')
PARM      KWD(WKOUTQ) TYPE(*NAME) LEN(10) MIN(1) +
          CHOICE(*NONE) PROMPT('Printer Output Queue')
PARM      KWD(RQSTR) TYPE(*CHAR) LEN(10) CHOICE('Your +
          Name') PROMPT('Requester')
PARM      KWD(COPIES) TYPE(*DEC) LEN(2) DFT(1) +
          RANGE(01 99) CHOICE(*VALUES) +
          PROMPT('Number of Copies')
```

Figure 1.3 shows the prompt screen that this command generates. Notice how the CMD statement in the source code determines the screen heading (Competitor Master File Listing). The heading also automatically includes the command name in parentheses following the text. The existence of the PARM statements in this example is what forces the prompt screen. Chapter 2 covers the PARM statement.

The four simple command statements in the source member above are all you need to create the screen shown in Figure 1.3. One interesting feature is that the function keys are displayed at the bottom of the screen. The system displays and processes them automatically; you do not have to do a thing. A command has certain features that cause some different function keys to be displayed and enabled, but all the function they represent (e.g., exit, prompt, refresh) is automatically built into every command you create.

Figure 1.3 Prompt Screen Generated by Command SA301CMD

```
                    Competitor Master File Listing (SA301CMD)

 Type choices, press Enter.

 Printer Output Queue . . . . . .
 Requester. . . . . . . . . . . .       _____     Your Name
 Number of Copies . . . . . . . .     1__              01-99




                                                                      Bottom
 F3=Exit    F4=Prompt    F5=Refresh    F12=Cancel    F13=How to use this display
 F24=More keys
```

Defining Parameters

Chapter 2

*The PARM statement
enables the command
prompt screen for up to 75
parameters.*

The most powerful use of commands is as a prompting tool. Commands
can generate a prompt screen requesting parameters, define the
description and the valid choices for each parameter, specify a default
value, perform basic editing on the values entered, and define
relationships among parameters. The second command definition
statement we will cover, the PARM statement, makes all this possible.
The PARM statement lets you define up to 75 parameters in a command.
You use one PARM statement per parameter. The PARM statement's
keywords describe the attributes of the PARM, such as length and prompt
text. This type of specification is analogous to how DDS defines the
characteristics of a field. Table 2.1 lists some of the more common
PARM statement keywords.

Table 2.1 Common PARM Keywords

PARM Statement Keywords	
TYPE	Specifies the data type of the parameter
LEN	Specifies the length of the parameter (and decimals, if numeric)
PROMPT	Specifies the text that is displayed to left of the input field
CHOICE	Specifies the choice text that is displayed to right of the input field
KWD	(Keyword) specifies the field name used for the PARM
DFT	Specifies the default value
MIN	Specifies the minimum number of values (used to make the PARM mandatory)
VALUES	Restricts input to these specified values
RANGE	Restricts input to this specified range of values
REL	Tests for a specified relationship

PARM Example

Let's begin with the example from Chapter 1 and look at the PARM
statements to see what function they serve.

Figure 2.1 Prompt Screen Generated by Command SA301CMD

```
                    Competitor Master File Listing (SA301CMD)

Type choices, press Enter.

Printer output queue . . . . . .     _____
Requester. . . . . . . . . . .      _____      Your Name
Number of copies . . . . . . .    1__             01-99














                                                                  Bottom
F3=Exit   F4=Prompt   F5=Refresh   F12=Cancel   F13=How to use this display
F24=More keys
```

The command in Figure 2.1 is prompting for three parameters, the
Printer output queue, the **Requester**, and the **Number of copies**, which
the competitor master file listing program needs. The following code
sample shows the command statements that created this prompt screen:

```
CMD       PROMPT('Competitor Master File Listing')
PARM      KWD(WKOUTQ) TYPE(*NAME) LEN(20) MIN(1) +
            CHOICE(*NONE) PROMPT('Printer Output Queue')
PARM      KWD(RQSTR) TYPE(*CHAR) LEN(210) MIN(1) +
            CHOICE('Your Name') PROMPT('Requester')
PARM      KWD(COPIES) TYPE(*DEC) LEN(2) DFT(1) +
            RANGE (01 99) CHOICE(*VALUES) +
            PROMPT('Number of Copies')
```

PARM Keywords

We've already discussed the CMD statement. Its PROMPT keyword
defines the screen heading for the prompt screen. The PARM statements
have more keywords. You use these keywords, whose descriptions
follow, to describe the parameters that appear on the screen.

KWD   All three PARM statements use KWD (keyword) to
designate the parameter's field name. For example, the

first PARM statement defines the keyword WKOUTQ for the printer output queue. You can see the keywords for each parameter on any command display by pressing F11. Keywords take on more importance when you use some of the advanced command functions that require referencing specific parameters.

TYPE The first PARM in this example, WKOUTQ, has its TYPE designated as *NAME, which means that it must conform to the AS/400 object-naming conventions. The first character must be alphabetic (A-Z, $, #, or @), and the remaining characters may be alphanumeric. The second PARM, RQSTR, is defined as TYPE(*CHAR), for character. The third PARM, COPIES, is defined as a numeric field with a length of 2 and 0 decimals. (We'll look at the rules about defining length in the next keyword.) These parameter types are very similar to using DDS data types to define a field's attributes. However, the command parameter types offer much more power and flexibility. Some of the valid TYPES are

> *CHAR — Character
>
> *DEC — Decimal
>
> *DATE - Date
>
> *NAME — System object name
>
> *GENERIC — Wild card value, ends in *

A special feature of the keyword TYPE is its automatic editing. The system will edit a parameter specified as TYPE(*DATE) for a valid date. The *NAME type will ensure that the value conforms to AS/400 object-naming conventions.

Appendix B lists all the valid parameter types.

There are many other, esoteric, parameter types, some of which we will discuss later. See Appendix B, "Parameter Types," for an extensive list.

LEN LEN (length) specifies the length of parameters defined in TYPE as *CHAR, *DEC, and *GENERIC. If the field is numeric, you define the number of decimals after the field length with one separating blank. Numeric fields will default to 0 decimals if not defined.

PROMPT The PROMPT keyword determines the prompt text that appears to the left of the input field. Notice how the command automatically centers the input field on the screen and places ellipses (. . .) between the end of the prompt text and the beginning of the input field. You may use a message file instead of constant prompt text. In that case, the message identifier is entered for the PROMPT value. Message files for PROMPT text are useful where the same PARMs occur frequently in an application (for example, all report requests use the PARM for printer output queue), because they provide consistency across all the screens. We discuss this feature in Chapter 7, "Message Files."

MIN

To make a parameter mandatory, specify MIN(1).

The MIN keyword shows the minimum number of values for the parameter. A value of 0 means that the parameter is optional. A value of 1 means that the parameter is required. Values greater than 1 are used for lists, which we discuss in Chapter 3, "Using Lists."

All required parameter statements must precede all optional parameter statements.

The first two parameters in our example have a MIN value of 1, which means they are required. If the user does not enter any value in these parameters, an error message will appear that states, "Parameter *xxxx* Required" (where *xxxx* is the keyword for the PARM). *All required parameter statements must precede all optional parameter statements.* If you do not follow this rule, the parameters will not be processed as mandatory parameters. Because mandatory parameters should logically appear before optional parameters for ease and speed of entry, this rule is not restrictive. However, if you do not want your required parameters to appear first on the prompt screen, you can use a relative prompt number on the PROMPT keyword (which we will demonstrate in the next example).

DFT

The DFT (default) keyword is used on the COPIES PARM statement. The value of 1 is displayed on the prompt screen. The user may change this value; otherwise, the value passed to the CPP will be the default value. The value for the default must conform to the length and type specified for the PARM.

RANGE

The RANGE keyword is used on the third PARM (COPIES) to restrict the valid values to between 01 and 99 (the RANGE keyword of the PARM command statement acts just like the DDS field-level keyword, RANGE). If the user enters a value less than 01 or greater than 99, an error message is displayed that states, "Range of parameter COPIES does not include *xx*" (where *xx* is the invalid value the user entered).

You can use the RANGE keyword with character-type and decimal-type PARMs.

CHOICE The CHOICE keyword determines the text that appears to the right of the input field. Generally, this text displays possible values or helps the user understand what value to enter for the parameter. The PARM WKOUTQ uses *NONE to indicate that no text is to be displayed. The PARM RQSTR specifies the text ("Your Name") to appear. The PARM COPIES uses the default, *VALUES. *VALUES will display each possible value, based on the PARM type, defaults, ranges, special values, etc. If there are more values than will fit on the line, the last value to fit will be followed by ellipses (. . .). Using F4 will display the entire list of values. You can also use message files for CHOICE text, just as you can for the PROMPT text. Another option for the CHOICE text is to specify a program that will dynamically retrieve the choice values and display them (see Chapter 11, "Choice Exit Programs").

Processing the Parameters

It's one thing to collect the information from the user and edit it to make sure it is valid, but what do you do with it? The CPP, the program that you specify in the CRTCMD command, receives the parameters and uses them for its work (see Figure 2.2).

Figure 2.2 Defining and Passing Parameters

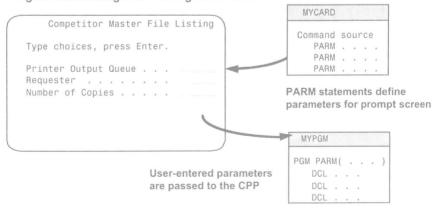

PARM statements define parameters for prompt screen

User-entered parameters are passed to the CPP

Let's look at the CL program that is the CPP for our example prompt:

```
PGM          PARM(&OUTQ &REQUESTER &COPIES)
/* DECLARE PROGRAM VARIABLES */
          DCL       VAR(&OUTQ) TYPE(*CHAR) LEN(10)
          DCL       VAR(&REQUESTER) TYPE(*CHAR) LEN(10)
          DCL       VAR(&COPIES) TYPE(*CHAR) LEN(2)
          DCL       VAR(&JOBTYPE) TYPE(*CHAR) LEN(1)
```

```
/* IF JOB IS INTERACTIVE VERSION, THEN SUBMIT IT */
          RTVJOBA   TYPE(&JOBTYPE)
          IF        COND(&JOBTYPE *EQ '1') THEN(DO)
          SBMJOB    CMD(CALL PGM(SA301C) PARM(&OUTQ &REQUESTER +
                    &COPIES)) JOB(SA301C) JOBQ(QBATCH) HOLD(*YES)
          SNDPGMMSG MSG('Competitor Master File Listing has been +
                    submitted on Hold') MSGTYPE(*INFO)
          GOTO      CMDLBL(END)
          ENDDO

/* OPEN DATA PATH BY ALPHA SORT NAME */
          OVRDBF    FILE(SACOMP) SHARE(*YES)
          OPNQRYF   FILE((SACOMP)) KEYFLD((SCALPH))

/* CALL PRINT PROGRAM */
          OVRPRTF   FILE(SA301A) TOFILE(QSYSPRT) OUTQ(&OUTQ) +
                    COPIES(&COPIES) USRDTA(&REQUESTER)
          CALL      PGM(SA301E) PARM(&REQUESTER)

          RCLRSC
END:      ENDPGM
```

The CL program above begins with a list of parameters that the
command has passed to it. You declare these parameters in the DCL
statements. The length of each parameter is the same as it was defined in
the command. Notice that the PARM types supported by commands map
to complementary data types supported by the CPP; for example, the
WKOUTQ parameter, which was TYPE(*NAME) in the command
source, became TYPE(*CHAR) LEN(10) in the CL source. Once the
parameters are in the CL program, it can go about its business, just as if
the user passed the parameters directly. This program uses the
information supplied in the parameters in a print file override and as data
passed to the print program.

Another Example

The first simple example showed the use of three keywords of the
PARM command definition statement. These are some of the most
commonly used keywords, used here in their simplest form. Let's
analyze another example that illustrates some additional PARM
keywords. Look at Figure 2.3.

Figure 2.3 Prompt Screen Generated by Command POPPVCMD

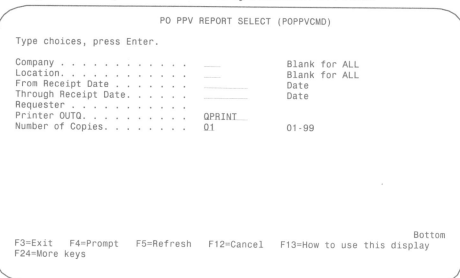

```
                        PO PPV REPORT SELECT (POPPVCMD)

Type choices, press Enter.

Company . . . . . . . . . . . . .    ___         Blank for ALL
Location. . . . . . . . . . . .      ___         Blank for ALL
From Receipt Date . . . . . . .      _____    Date
Through Receipt Date. . . . . .      _____    Date
Requester . . . . . . . . . . .
Printer OUTQ. . . . . . . . . .      QPRINT
Number of Copies. . . . . . . .      01           01-99




                                                                     Bottom
 F3=Exit   F4=Prompt   F5=Refresh   F12=Cancel   F13=How to use this display
 F24=More keys
```

The display shown in Figure 2.3 prompts the user for information
required to run a purchase price variance report. The following code
shows the command statements for the POPPVCMD command.

```
CMD         PROMPT('PO PPV REPORT SELECT')
PARM        KWD(FRDATE) TYPE(*DATE) REL(*LE &TODATE) +
              MIN(1) PROMPT('From Receipt Date' 3)
PARM        KWD(TODATE) TYPE(*DATE) REL(GE &FRDATE) +
              MIN(1) PROMPT('Through Receipt Date' 4)
PARM        KWD(CO) TYPE(*CHAR) LEN(3) CHOICE('Blank +
              for ALL') PROMPT('Company' 1)
PARM        KWD(LOC) TYPE(*CHAR) LEN(3) CHOICE('Blank for +
              ALL') PROMPT('Location' 2)
PARM        KWD(REQST) TYPE(*CHAR) LEN(120) CHOICE(*NONE) +
              PROMPT('Requester')
PARM        KWD(OUTQ) TYPE(*CHAR) LEN(10) DFT(QPRINT) +
              CHOICE(*NONE) PROMPT('Printer OITQ')
PARM        KWD(COPY) TYPE(*CHAR) LEN(2) DFT(01) +
              RANGE(01 99) PROMPT('Number of Copies')
```

The user can specify seven different parameters when requesting this
report. We've seen most of these PARM keywords before, but there are
three new twists. The first is a new TYPE keyword value, *DATE; the
second is the REL keyword; and the third is the relative prompt number.

TYPE(*DATE) The first two PARMs in the source member,
FRDATE and TODATE, are specified as type *DATE.
They will be edited automatically for validity. If the
user enters the wrong date, an error message appears:
"Value '999999' for parameter FRDATE not a valid

date" (where '999999' represents the invalid value the user entered). Keep in mind that the user enters the date in the system format specified by the system value of QDATFMT (generally MMDDYY), but *the date value passed to the CPP is in the format CYYMMDD*. The century digit is assumed to be 0 (20th century) if the year is between 40 and 99 (1940 through 1999), inclusive. The century digit is assumed to be 1 (21st century) if the year is between 0 and 39 (2000 through 2039), inclusive.

The user enters the date in the system format, but the date value passed to the CPP is in the format CYYMMDD.

It is important to understand that the command passes the date to the CPP in CYYMMDD format. If the command passes the date to the CPP in CYYMMDD format (for example, 0941231) and the CPP is expecting it to be in MMDDYY format (for example, 123194), the CPP will interpret the year as the month, the month as the day, and the day as the year. If the CPP in our example were coded incorrectly, it would try to process the date as the 12th day of the 94th month of the 31st year. To quote IBM, certainly "unpredictable results will occur" in this case.

When entering data into a *DATE PARM, the user may or may not use date-separator characters. The system value QDATSEP determines the date-separator character (generally, /). It does not matter whether the users enter separators; either approach is acceptable to the command. This flexibility lets users enter the date in the format they find most comfortable.

The REL keyword enforces relationships between command parameters and, optionally, constants.

REL

The REL keyword is new to this discussion. Both of the date PARMs, FRDATE and TODATE, use REL to specify a relationship. Because a *from date* and a *to date* are requested, the *from date* must be less than or equal to the *to date* and the *to date* must be greater than or equal to the *from date*. The REL keyword enforces this relationship. If a user enters values that do not meet the specified relationship, an error message appears: "Value for FRDATE must be less than or equal to TODATE." You can specify either a constant or PARM keyword in defining a relationship. Note that when you use a keyword (as in our example), you must precede it with an ampersand character (&). *All PARM statements using the REL keyword must precede all other PARM statements.* If you don't follow this rule, the relationship will not be enforced.

Specifying a relative prompt number lets you alter the order of the parameters on the screen.

Relative Prompt Number The last new function is the relative prompt number. Notice that the order of the PARM statements in the source is not the same as the order in which the parameters appear on the prompt screen. Because all parm statements using MIN(1) and REL must appear first in the source, you specify the relative prompt number on the PROMPT keyword to change the display order (the relative prompt number is the second, optional value in the PROMPT keyword). For example, the PARM for CO is first because the relative prompt number is 1. All PARMs having relative prompt numbers appear first, in relative prompt number order. Then all other PARMs are displayed in the order in which they appear in the source.

The CPP receives parameters in the same order that they appear in the command source.

It is important to know that the sequence of the PARMs in the source member, not their display sequence, determines the order in which PARMs are passed to the CPP. This point is critical, because the CPP processes those parameters in the order in which they are passed. The following sample code shows the CL program that is the CPP for this command:

```
PGM            PARM(&FR &TO &CO &LOC &REQUESTER &OUTQ &COPIES)
```

```
/*DECLARE PROGRAM VARIABLES   */
            DCL         VAR(&CO) TYPE(*CHAR) LEN(3)
            DCL         VAR(&LOC) TYPE(*CHAR) LEN(3)
            DCL         VAR(&FR) TYPE(*CHAR) LEN(7)
            DCL         VAR(&TO) TYPE(*CHAR) LEN(7)
            DCL         VAR(&REQUESTER) TYPE(*CHAR) LEN(10)
            DCL         VAR(&OUTQ) TYPE(*CHAR) LEN(10)
            DCL         VAR(&COPIES) TYPE(*CHAR) LEN(2)
              .
              .
              .
/* CALL THE RPG PRINT PROGRAM */
            CALL        PGM(POPPVE) PARM(&CO &LOC &FR &TO +
                            &REQUESTER)

/* RECLAIM RESOURCES */
            RCLRSC

END:        ENDPGM
```

It is critical that you know the sequence of the parameters and that the sequence is consistent between the command and the CPP. For example, if the CPP expected the values based on their appearance on the screen, the order would be CO, LOC, FR, TO, REQUESTER, OUTQ, and COPIES. But the command actually passes them according to the source sequence; that is, FR, TO, CO, LOC, REQUESTER, OUTQ, and

COPIES. In this case, the value of FR is in the CPP's parameter for CO and LOC, the value of TO overlaps into other parameters, and so on.

Using Lists

Chapter 3

Lists allow multiple values for a single parameter. IBM-supplied commands frequently use lists, which can add a richness of functionality to your commands. Lists can add a degree of sophistication to your commands. They enable your prompt screens to display parameters in an organized, meaningful way, making them more user friendly. The three types of lists are simple lists, mixed lists, and compound lists (a list within a list).

Simple Lists

Simple lists allow multiple values of the same type for a single command parameter.

A simple list is a single parameter containing one or more values of the same type, such as libraries, objects, or application codes. Let's look at an IBM-supplied command that uses a simple list. Figure 3.1 represents IBM's RSTOBJ (Restore Object) command. The first parameter, **Objects**, is a simple list. You can tell because of the + **for more values** prompt, which indicates that you can enter one or more values. The **Device** parameter and **Object types** parameter are also simple lists. When you enter a +, the number of input fields displayed expands to let you enter all the elements of the list (Figure 3.2). All the values entered in the list must comply with the attributes specified for the PARM (e.g., length, type).

Figure 3.1 RSTOBJ Command Illustrating a Simple List

```
                         Restore Object (RSTOBJ)

Type choices, press Enter.
Objects . . . . . . . . . . . .    TESTLIB       Name, generic*, *ALL
           + for more values       +
Saved library . . . . . . . .                    Name
Device. . . . . . . . . . . .                    Name, *SAVF
           + for more values
Object types. . . . . . . . .      *ALL           *ALL, *ALRTBL, *CFGL...
           + for more values




                                                              Bottom
F3=Exit    F4=Prompt   F5=Refresh   F10=Additional parameters  F12=Cancel
F13=How to use this display        F24=More keys
```

Figure 3.2 RSTOBJ Command (Simple List), Expanded OBJ Parameter

```
                    Specify More Values for Parameter OBJ

Type choices, press Enter.
Objects . . . . . . . . . . . .    TESTLIB       Name, generic*, *ALL
                                   _____
                                   _____
                                   _____
                                   _____
                                   _____
                                   _____
                                   _____
                                   _____
                                   _____
                                   _____
                                   _____

                                                              More...
F3=Exit    F4=Prompt   F5=Refresh   F12=Cancel   F13=How to use this display
F24=More keys
```

Let's look at a custom application example. Figure 3.3 and the sample code that follows illustrate a simple list in a user-defined command. This command prompts the user for information needed to run a report that shows inventory adjustments by reason code. Sometimes, users may want a single adjustment code; but other times, they might want to select multiple codes. The simple list provides that capability without extensive programming.

Figure 3.3 Prompt Screen Generated by Command IA521CMD

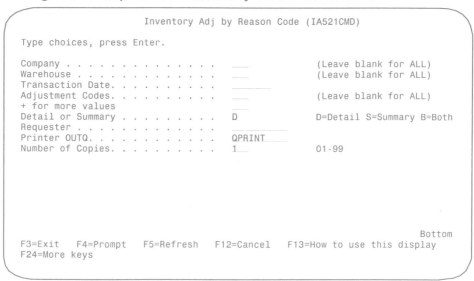

```
                    Inventory Adj by Reason Code (IA521CMD)

Type choices, press Enter.

Company . . . . . . . . . . . . . . .    ___        (Leave blank for ALL)
Warehouse . . . . . . . . . . . . .      ___        (Leave blank for ALL)
Transaction Date. . . . . . . . . .      _____
Adjustment Codes. . . . . . . . . .      ___        (Leave blank for ALL)
+ for more values                        ___
Detail or Summary . . . . . . . . .      D          D=Detail S=Summary B=Both
Requester . . . . . . . . . . . . .      _____
Printer OUTQ. . . . . . . . . . . .      QPRINT____
Number of Copies. . . . . . . . . .      1__        01-99




                                                                       Bottom
F3=Exit    F4=Prompt    F5=Refresh    F12=Cancel    F13=How to use this display
F24=More keys
```

On this screen, the users can specify the transactions they want, including multiple adjustment codes. If users key a + in **+ for more values**, the command will display another screen that lets them enter multiple adjustment codes.

The following code shows the command statements that produced the screen in Figure 3.3:

```
CMD         PROMPT('Inventory Adj by Reason Code')
PARM        KWD(WKDATE) TYPE(*DATE) MIN(1) CHOICE(*NONE) +
              PROMPT('Transaction Date' 3)
PARM        KWD(WKREQ) TYPE(*CHAR) LEN(10) MIN(1) +
              CHOICE(*NONE) PROMPT('Requester' 6)
PARM        KWD(WKCO) TYPE(*CHAR) LEN(3) MIN(0) +
              CHOICE('(Leave blank for ALL)') +
              PROMPT('Company' 1)
PARM        KWD(WKWH) TYPE(*CHAR) LEN(3) MIN(0) +
              CHOICE('(Leave blank for ALL)') +
              PROMPT('Warehouse' 2)
PARM        KWD(WKADJ) TYPE(*CHAR) LEN(2) MIN(0) MAX(10) +
              CHOICE('(Leave blank for ALL)') +
              PROMPT('Adjustment Codes' 4)
PARM        KWD(WKDS) TYPE(*CHAR) LEN(1) RSTD(*YES) +
              DFT(D) VALUES(D S B) MIN(0) +
              CHOICE('D=Detail S=Summary B=Both') +
              PROMPT('Detail or Summary' 5)
```

```
PARM        KWD(WKOUTQ) TYPE(*CHAR) LEN(10) DFT(QPRINT) +
              CHOICE(*NONE) PROMPT('Printer OUTQ')
PARM        KWD(WKCOPY) TYPE(*CHAR) LEN(2) DFT(1) +
              RANGE(01 99) PROMPT('Number of Copies')
```

The MAX keyword determines the maximum number of values in a list PARM.

A single keyword gives us the capability of the simple list. To specify a simple list, use the MAX keyword on the PARM statement. The value of the MAX keyword determines the maximum number of values the list may contain. All values in the list will have the attributes of the PARM statement.

The **Adjustment Codes** parameter lets you select up to 10 adjustment codes (as determined by the MAX keyword for the PARM WKADJ) to include on the report. All values entered (up to 10) must conform to the attributes of that PARM statement; that is, type must be character, and length must be 2. All that is required to turn a PARM into a simple list is to specify a value for the MAX keyword that is greater than 1, as in this example, where MAX is 10.

The processing of a list takes special code in the CPP. We will show you how to manage lists in the CPP later in this chapter.

To restrict a parameter's values, use the RSTD keyword.

In the above example, we see two new PARM keywords that give us additional editing capabilities. The WKDS (**Detail or Summary**) PARM is prompting for detail, summary, or both. Notice how the VALUES keyword is used to limit the entry to **D**, **S**, or **B**. When using VALUES, you must also use the RSTD (Restricted) keyword with a value of *YES. The *YES on the RSTD keyword restricts entry of the PARM to the values specified on the VALUES keyword.

Mixed Lists

A mixed list is a set of separately defined elements for a single parameter. Again, we'll begin with an IBM example to illustrate this concept.

To define a mixed list, use the ELEM statement.

Figure 3.4 shows a section of the prompting for IBM's CHGJOBD (Change Job Description) command. The **Message logging:** parameter is a mixed list. It contains three elements (level, severity, and text). Each element has different attributes (prompt, length, type, choice) because each element is individually defined. Notice how the prompt text of the individual elements is indented beneath the prompt text of the PARM itself.

The ELEM command statement, the third of the six command definition statements, defines mixed lists.

Figure 3.4 CHGJOB Command (Mixed List), MSGLOG Parameter

```
                            Change Job Description (CHGJOBD)

 Type choices, press Enter.

 Accounting code . . . . . . . . . .   *SAME
 Routing data. . . . . . . . . . . .   *SAME

 Request data or command . . . . . .   *SAME



 CL syntax check . . . . . . . . . .   *SAME          0-99, *SAME, *NOCHK
 Initial library list. . . . . . . .   *SAME          Name, *SAME, *SYSVAL, *NONE
                 + for more values
 End severity. . . . . . . . . . . .   *SAME          0-99, *SAME
 Message logging:
   Level . . . . . . . . . . . . . .   *SAME          0-4, *SAME
   Severity. . . . . . . . . . . . .   *SAME          0-99, *SAME
   Text. . . . . . . . . . . . . . .   *SAME          *SAME, *MSG, *SECLVL, *NOLIST
 Log CL program comments . . . . . .   *SAME          *SAME, *NO, *YES
                                                                         More...
 F3=Exit    F4=Prompt    F5=Refresh    F12=Cancel    F13=How to use this display
 F24=More keys
```

Elements in a mixed list may have different attributes.

The main reason for using a mixed list instead of a simple list is that the mixed list allows the elements of the list to have different attributes, because they are separately defined. You can define those different elements as individual PARMs instead, but a mixed list is often better. One good reason to use a mixed list is that the elements of a mixed list appear indented under a heading, which can improve the readability of the screen by indicating to the user that those parameters are related to each other.

A final reason for choosing a mixed list over a simple list (all other things being equal) is because a mixed list is actually a little easier to process in the CPP. The section on processing lists later in this chapter will examine this point.

Let's examine a custom command that uses the ELEM command statement to define a mixed list. First, look at the prompt screen in Figure 3.5. The first parameter, **Select reports with an X**, is a mixed list. It consists of six separately defined elements (the six elements indented beneath it). We know that they are separately defined because they have different prompt texts, and there is no **+ for more values** that the simple list uses.

Figure 3.5 Command SA102CMD, Mixed List Example

```
                        Monthly Sales Reports (SA102CMD)

 Type choices, press Enter.

 Select Reports with an X:
   Cust Summary Prod Line SA102A        _
   Slsmn Summary Prod Line SA102B       _
   Terr Summary Prod Line SA102C        _
   Mrkt Summary Prod Line SA102D        _
   Customer Summary - SA102E . .        _
   Salesman Summary - SA102F . .        _
 Select Month/Year . . . . . . .        ____    MMYY
 Division . . . . . . . . . . . .        _      (Blank for ALL Div)
 Market . . . . . . . . . . . . .        _      (Blank for ALL Markets)
 Territory. . . . . . . . . . . .        ____   (Blank for ALL Territories)
 Salesman . . . . . . . . . . . .        ____   (Blank for ALL Salesmen)
 Customer Group . . . . . . . . .        ____   (Blank for ALL Groups)
 Customer * . . . . . . . . . . .        ____   Blank for ALL Customers
 Requester. . . . . . . . . . . .
 Printer OUTQ . . . . . . . . .         QPRINT____
                                                                 More...
 F3=Exit  F4=Prompt  F5=Refresh  F12=Cancel  F13=How to use this display
 F24=More keys
```

Now look at the source code shown below for that PARM
(RPTLIST). The PARM type is not *CHAR, *DEC, or any value we
have previously seen. The TYPE of RPTELEM is simply a name (a
statement label) that references the ELEM command statements that
make up the mixed list. The six ELEM statements for RPTLIST are at
the end of the source member, specified by the label RPTELEM.

The ELEM command statement is very similar to the PARM
statement in that it defines parameters, but these parameters are elements
of a mixed list. ELEM even uses many of the same keywords as the
PARM statement, such as TYPE, LEN, DFT, VALUES, REL, RANGE,
MIN, PROMPT, and CHOICE (see Appendix D for a more extensive list
of ELEM statement keywords).

In our example, all six elements of the mixed list are character fields
with a length of 1. Their values are restricted to X or blank. Each has a
different prompt text specified.

```
          CMD        PROMPT('Monthly Sales Reports')
          PARM       KWD(RPTLIST) TYPE(RPTELEM) MIN(1) MAX(1) +
          PROMPT('Select Reports with an X')
                       .
                       .
                       .
RPTELEM:  ELEM       TYPE(*CHAR) LEN(1) RSTD(*YES)  VALUES(X ' ') +
                       MIN(0) CHOICE(*NONE) +
                       PROMPT('Cust Summary Prod Line SA102A')
          ELEM       TYPE(*CHAR) LEN(1) RSTD(*YES) VALUES(X ' ') +
```

```
                             MIN(0) CHOICE(*NONE) +
                             PROMPT('Slsmn Summary Prod Line SA102B')
             ELEM            TYPE(*CHAR) LEN(1) RSTD(*YES) VALUES(X ' ') +
                             MIN(0) CHOICE(*NONE) +
                             PROMPT('Terr Summary Prod Line SA102C')
             ELEM            TYPE(*CHAR) LEN(1) RSTD(*YES) VALUES(X ' ') +
                             MIN(0) CHOICE(*NONE) +
                             PROMPT('Mrkt Summary Prod Line SA102D')
             ELEM            TYPE(*CHAR) LEN(1) RSTD(*YES) VALUES(X ' ') +
                             MIN(0) CHOICE(*NONE) +
                             PROMPT('Customer Summary - SA102E')
```

This example does not require a mixed list. We could have defined these six elements as six different PARMs. But we used a mixed list to group these six parameters, indented under a single heading, to make it easier to understand that these six parameters are related to each other.

Use mixed lists to group and isolate parameters under a common prompt.

In fact, no situation demands the use of a mixed list. The mixed list is a way to isolate a group of parameters by indenting them under a common prompt. It is more a visual matter than a system requirement. You might want to use a mixed list to define a general ledger account number that is broken into parts: the general heading of G/L number, with each individual part defined as company, department, account number.

Notice the word **More...** in the lower right corner of the screen in Figure 3.5. This word indicates that the prompt continues on the next screen, which you access by pressing the Page-Down key. The command adds this function automatically because all the parameters do not fit on one screen. The last PARM, COPY, will appear after you press the Page-Down key.

Compound Lists

Compound lists are lists within lists. You'll use them less frequently than simple or mixed lists. A compound list may be a list that you specify more than once for a parameter. For example, a user might need multiple ranges of general ledger account numbers to be included in a report. Each set of ranges is a list, and the list of those lists is a compound list. We will show you an example of this type of compound list later in this section.

A compound list can also be a list you specify for an element in a mixed list. Another example from a G/L application might be a prompt requesting a multi-part general ledger account number (company/department/general ledger number), but the user can enter a list of G/L numbers within the company and department.

An IBM example will help illustrate the concept of compound lists. Figure 3.6 shows the IBM command ADDBKP (Add Breakpoint), used in debugging. The first parameter, **Statement identifier ❶**, is a simple list (indicated by the **+ for more values** prompt). The second parameter, **Program variables: ❷**, at first appears to be a mixed list because it has two separately defined elements (**Program variable** and **Basing pointer variable**). However, ❷ is really a compound list because you can specify the entire mixed list parameter more than once (**❸ , + for more values**). ❷ also contains a simple list specified for an element (**Basing pointer variable**) in a mixed list (**❹, + for more values**) so ❷ actually meets both definitions of a compound list.

Figure 3.6 ADDBKP Command, Illustrating Compound Lists

```
                        Add Breakpoint (ADDBKP)

    Type choices, press Enter.

❶ Statement identifier . . . . . .              _____      Character value
                     + for more values          _____
    Program variables:
❷   Program variable . . . . . . .     *NONE_____
    _____

    Basing pointer variable. . . . .      _____
    _____

❹                  + for more values      _

❸                  + for more values      _
    Output format. . . . . . . . . .      *CHAR        *CHAR, *HEX
    Program. . . . . . . . . . . . .      *DFTPGM____  Name, *DFTPGM

                                                                Bottom
    F3=Exit   F4=Prompt   F5=Refresh   F10=Additional parameters   F12=Cancel
    F13=How to use this display        F24=More keys
```

Your application uses for compound lists will probably not be quite this exotic. Figure 3.7 shows a custom example using a compound list. This prompt screen requests information to run a general ledger report. The user may request a range of G/L account numbers. This range is set up as a mixed list. We define each element separately because we need different PROMPT values for each one (**From account number** is the first element, and **To account number** is the second element). If users want to request more than one range, they may do so because they can specify this mixed list more than once by placing a **+** in the appropriate prompt field (which results in the screen shown in Figure 3.8). This example is a compound list because it uses a mixed list that you may specify more than once.

Figure 3.7 Application Example of a Compound List

```
                    GL Account Report Listing (GLACCTCMD)

Type choices, press Enter.

Account Number Range:
  From Account . . . . . . . . . .    005000      Character value
  To Account . . . . . . . . . . .    006000      Character value
              + for more values       +
Requester. . . . . . . . . . . . .    _____
Printer Output Queue . . . . . . .    QPRINT____
Number of Copies . . . . . . . . .    1_          01-99




                                                              Bottom
F3=Exit    F4=Prompt    F5=Refresh    F12=Cancel   F13=How to use this display
F24=More keys
```

Figure 3.8 Custom Example of Compound List, List Expanded

```
                    Specify More Values for Parameter ACCT

Type choices, press Enter.

Account Number Range:
  From Account . . . . . . . . . .    005000      Character value
  To Account . . . . . . . . . . .    006000      Character value

  From Account . . . . . . . . . .    _____      Character value
  To Account . . . . . . . . . . .    _____      Character value

  From Account . . . . . . . . . .    _____      Character value
  To Account . . . . . . . . . . .    _____      Character value

  From Account . . . . . . . . . .    _____      Character value
  To Account . . . . . . . . . . .    _____      Character value

  From Account . . . . . . . . . .    _____      Character value
  To Account . . . . . . . . . . .    _____      Character value
                                                              Bottom
F3=Exit    F4=Prompt  F5=Refresh    F12=Cancel   F13=How to use this display
F24=More keys
```

To create a compound list, simply define a mixed list and specify a MAX value greater than one. In effect, make the mixed list a simple list, as shown on the following page in the source code for a compound list. You define the account range parameters as a mixed list by using the ELEM statements to individually describe the two parameters (**From**

Account and **To Account**). Then, on the PARM statement, you set the MAX keyword to 5. Now, the user can specify the mixed list up to five times.

```
CMD         PROMPT('GL Account Report Listing')
            PARM        KWD(WKREQ) TYPE(*CHAR) LEN(10) MIN(1) +
                        CHOICE(*NONE) PROMPT('Requester' 2)
            PARM        KWD(ACCT) TYPE(ELEM1) MAX(5) +
                        PROMPT('Account Number Range' 1)
            PARM        KWD(WKOUTQ) TYPE(*CHAR) LEN(10) DFT(QPRINT) +
                        CHOICE(*NONE) PROMPT('Printer Output Queue')
            PARM        KWD(WKCOPY) TYPE(*CHAR) LEN(2) DFT(1) +
                        RANGE(01 99) MIN(0) PROMPT('Number of +
                        Copies')
ELEM1:      ELEM        TYPE(*CHAR) LEN(6) PROMPT('From Account')
            ELEM        TYPE(*CHAR) LEN(6) PROMPT('To Account')
```

Processing Lists

Processing a list in the CPP is not the same as processing regular parameters. Regular parameters are passed to the CPP exactly as they appear in the source. Lists are passed differently.

A list is passed to the CPP as a single parameter, with the number of list elements in the first two binary bytes.

A list is passed as one parameter, as you can see in Figure 3.9. The first two bytes of a list parameter contain the binary value of the number of elements passed. The remaining bytes are the elements in the list. This fact is very important to know so you can make the CPP process the values properly.

In a simple list, only the elements the user enters are passed to the CPP, so the binary value containing the number of elements passed is very important. You must use this value to determine which of the element values of the simple list to process. For example, a simple list containing up to 10 values might, in a given instance, have only three user-specified values designated. The binary value will be 3, and the three entered values will follow (the remaining bytes will contain garbage). In a mixed list, all elements are passed, so processing the binary value is not critical.

Processing Mixed Lists

Because mixed lists are less complex to process than simple lists, we will discuss a mixed list first. The sample code on the following page shows part of a CL program that is the CPP for the command SA102CMD (previously shown in Figure 3.5 and the related source code on pages 28 and 29), which prompts the user for up to six different sales reports. The parameter &RPTLIST represents a mixed list containing six elements of 1 byte each. In the CL program, the variable &RPTLIST is defined as 8 characters in length. That is six elements of 1 byte each, equaling 6 characters, plus the 2-byte binary prefix, which equals 8 bytes, as shown below.

The CPP for a mixed list parameter need not process the binary prefix; instead, start extracting all the list values beginning in position 3.

Because &RPTLIST is a mixed list and all the elements are passed, we do not have to process the binary prefix. However, we have to accommodate that prefix when extracting the individual elements from the list. As shown in the example, we create the first element of the list, &RPT1, by using the substring function to extract the values in &RPTLIST, beginning in position 3 for 1 byte. The values begin in position 3 because positions 1 and 2 contain the binary value of the number of elements in the list. We extract the other elements of the list (2 through 6) in the same manner.

Figure 3.9 A Mixed List Being Passed to a CL Program
RPTLIST

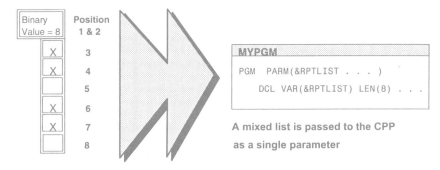

```
        PGM         PARM(&RPTLIST &WKMMYY &WKDIV &WKMRKT &WKTERR +
                         &WKSLMN &WKCGRP &WKCUST &WKREQ &WKOUTQ &WKCOPY)
/* DECLARE PROGRAM VARIABLES */
        DCL         VAR(&RPTLIST) TYPE(*CHAR) LEN(8)
        DCL         VAR(&RPT1) TYPE(*CHAR) LEN(1)
        DCL         VAR(&RPT2) TYPE(*CHAR) LEN(1)
        DCL         VAR(&RPT3) TYPE(*CHAR) LEN(1)
        DCL         VAR(&RPT4) TYPE(*CHAR) LEN(1)
        DCL         VAR(&RPT5) TYPE(*CHAR) LEN(1)
        DCL         VAR(&RPT6) TYPE(*CHAR) LEN(1)
/* SET UP PROGRAM VARIABLES */
        CHGVAR      VAR (&RPT1) VALUE (%SST (&RPTLIST 3 1))
        CHGVAR      VAR (&RPT2) VALUE (%SST (&RPTLIST 4 1))
        CHGVAR      VAR (&RPT3) VALUE (%SST (&RPTLIST 5 1))
        CHGVAR      VAR (&RPT4) VALUE (%SST (&RPTLIST 6 1))
        CHGVAR      VAR (&RPT5) VALUE (%SST (&RPTLIST 7 1))
        CHGVAR      VAR (&RPT6) VALUE (%SST (&RPTLIST 8 1))
```

Processing Simple Lists

The CPP for a simple list must process the binary prefix, to determine how many elements of the list were passed from the command.

Now let's look at an example of the code to process a simple list. Because the only elements of a simple list that are passed to the CPP are those that have values the user enters, you must process the 2-byte binary prefix to determine which variables to load with values. (Figure 3.10 illustrates this process.) The code that follows (page 35) shows part of a CL program that processes the simple list from our earlier example that requested inventory adjustment codes for the inventory adjustment by reason code report (see the sample code on pages 25 and 26).

Figure 3.10 A Simple List Passed to a CL Program

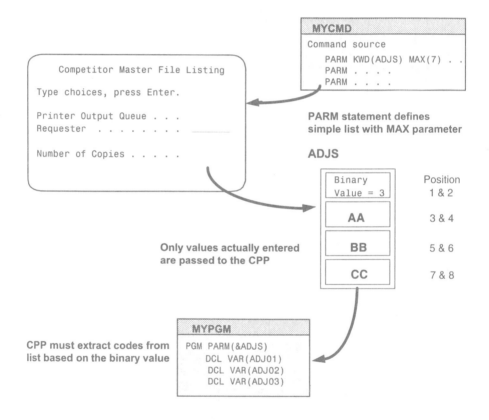

```
               PGM              PARM(&WKDATE7 &WKREQ &WKCO &WKWH &ADJLIST &WKDS +
                                &WKOUTQ &WKCOPY)

/* DECLARE PROGRAM VARIABLES */
               DCL              VAR(&WKCO) TYPE(*CHAR) LEN(3)       /* Company    */
               DCL              VAR(&WKWH) TYPE(*CHAR) LEN(3)       /* Warehouse  */
               DCL              VAR(&WKDATE7) TYPE(*CHAR) LEN(7)    /* DATE       */
               DCL              VAR(&ADJLIST) TYPE(*CHAR) LEN(22) /* List of +
                                                             Adjustment Codes */
               DCL              VAR(&WKDS) TYPE(*CHAR) LEN(1)       /* Dtl or Sum */
               DCL              VAR(&WKREQ) TYPE(*CHAR) LEN(10)     /* Requester  */
               DCL              VAR(&WKOUTQ) TYPE(*CHAR) LEN(10)    /* Outq       */
               DCL              VAR(&WKCOPY) TYPE(*CHAR) LEN(2)     /* Copies     */

/* DECLARE ELEMENTS OF ADJUSTMENT CODE LIST */
               DCL              VAR(&ADJ01) TYPE(*CHAR) LEN(2)       /* ADJ CODE 1 */
               DCL              VAR(&ADJ02) TYPE(*CHAR) LEN(2)       /* ADJ CODE 2 */
               DCL              VAR(&ADJ03) TYPE(*CHAR) LEN(2)       /* ADJ CODE 3 */
               DCL              VAR(&ADJ04) TYPE(*CHAR) LEN(2)       /* ADJ CODE 4 */
               DCL              VAR(&ADJ05) TYPE(*CHAR) LEN(2)       /* ADJ CODE 5 */
               DCL              VAR(&ADJ06) TYPE(*CHAR) LEN(2)       /* ADJ CODE 6 */
               DCL              VAR(&ADJ07) TYPE(*CHAR) LEN(2)       /* ADJ CODE 7 */
               DCL              VAR(&ADJ08) TYPE(*CHAR) LEN(2)       /* ADJ CODE 8 */
               DCL              VAR(&ADJ09) TYPE(*CHAR) LEN(2)       /* ADJ CODE 9 */
               DCL              VAR(&ADJ10) TYPE(*CHAR) LEN(2)       /* ADJ CODE 10*/
               DCL              &BIN *CHAR LEN(2) /* Number of ADJs in List +
                                                              - Binary */
               DCL              VAR(&DEC) TYPE(*DEC) LEN(5 0) /* Number of +
                                                        ADJs in List - Decimal */

/* SET UP ADJUSTMENT CODE VARIABLES */
               CHGVAR           &BIN %SST(&ADJLIST 1 2) /*Extract # of ADJs In +
                                                                         List*/
               CHGVAR           &DEC %BINARY(&BIN 1 2) /* Convert Binary to- +
                                                                    Decimal */

               IF               COND(&DEC *GE 01) THEN(CHGVAR VAR(&ADJ01) +
                                VALUE(%SST(&ADJLIST 3 2)))
               IF               COND(&DEC *GE 02) THEN(CHGVAR VAR(&ADJ02) +
                                VALUE(%SST(&ADJLIST 5 2)))
               IF               COND(&DEC *GE 03) THEN(CHGVAR VAR(&ADJ03) +
                                VALUE(%SST(&ADJLIST 7 2)))
               IF               COND(&DEC *GE 04) THEN(CHGVAR VAR(&ADJ04) +
                                VALUE(%SST(&ADJLIST 9 2)))
               IF               COND(&DEC *GE 05) THEN(CHGVAR VAR(&ADJ05) +
                                VALUE(%SST(&ADJLIST 11 2)))
               IF               COND(&DEC *GE 06) THEN(CHGVAR VAR(&ADJ06) +
                                VALUE(%SST(&ADJLIST 13 2)))
               IF               COND(&DEC *GE 07) THEN(CHGVAR VAR(&ADJ07) +
                                VALUE(%SST(&ADJLIST 15 2)))
               IF               COND(&DEC *GE 08) THEN(CHGVAR VAR(&ADJ08) +
                                VALUE(%SST(&ADJLIST 17 2)))
               IF               COND(&DEC *GE 09) THEN(CHGVAR VAR(&ADJ09) +
                                VALUE(%SST(&ADJLIST 19 2)))
               IF               COND(&DEC *GE 10) THEN(CHGVAR VAR(&ADJ10) +
                                VALUE(%SST(&ADJLIST 21 2)))
```

The variable &ADJLIST is a mixed list containing 10 elements of two characters each. Those elements, plus the 2-byte binary prefix, give the variable a length of 22. The program must extract the elements of &ADJLIST into individual parameters (&ADJ01, &ADJ02, etc.). After defining all variables, the program determines the value of the binary prefix by using CL's binary built-in function. Then the program loads the appropriate values to the individual variables.

If you ignore the value in the binary prefix when processing a simple list and attempt to extract the elements by assuming that the unused elements will contain blanks, you will get garbage values in the elements that the user did not enter. The unused parameters are actually filled with the values of the parameters that follow the simple list because they are in the buffer.

Processing Compound Lists

To process a compound list, the CPP must determine the number of lists, as well as the number of elements in each list.

Processing compound lists in the CPP is more complex than simple- or mixed-list processing. Like a simple or mixed list, a compound list is passed as one parameter. However, the first 2 bytes of a compound list contain the binary value of the *number of lists*, not the number of elements in the list. Following this are binary values defining the offset or displacement to each of the lists. These offset values tell you where in the parameter string each list starts. Then, after all the offset values, the lists of data begin. Figure 3.11 shows the basic structure of a compound list parameter.

Let's use the command shown in Figures 3.7 and 3.8 as an example. This example shows a compound list consisting of a mixed list that can occur up to five times. Each mixed list contains a 6-byte **From account number** and a 6-byte **To account number**. In our example, the user entered only the first list, indicating that account range 5000 through 6000 should be included on the report. This list parameter would be passed to the CPP as shown in Figure 3.12.

Figure 3.11 Compound List

Number of Lists 2 bytes (binary)
Offset to List 1 2 bytes (binary)
Offset to List 2 2 bytes (binary)
Offset to List 3 2 bytes (binary)
• •
• •
Offset to List X 2 bytes (binary)
List Data • • • •

Figure 3.12 Compound List Parameter Example

Starting Position of List

0001	0004	0002	005000	006000
Number of Lists 2 bytes (binary)	Offset to List 2 bytes (binary)	Number of Elems. 2 bytes (binary)	From Acct.	To Acct.

Mixed List

The first 2 bytes contain the binary value of the number of lists (only one in this example). The next 2 bytes (0004 in our example) give the offset value that points to the beginning of the list within the parameter. You start counting from the beginning of the parameter (remember, those binary values occupy 2 bytes). Four bytes from the first one takes us just to the start of the mixed list.

The mixed list appears in its usual format; that is, it is prefixed by a 2-byte binary value containing the number of elements in the mixed list (which will always be the number of elements defined in the command, since all elements of a mixed list are passed to the CPP).

Compound lists are passed to the CPP in reverse order, although the offset values are in correct order.

To complicate matters, the lists are not passed to the CPP in the order in which they appear on the screen, but in reverse order. In other words, if you enter list one, list two, and list three, they will be passed in this order: list three, list two, list one. However, the offset values are in order (e.g., first offset for list one, second offset for list two). An example will clarify this.

Let's still use the range of account numbers example shown in Figures 3.7 and 3.8. Assume this time, however, that the user enters the following values for three account number ranges:

- Range one   111111 – 222222
- Range two   333333 – 444444
- Range three   555555 – 666666

The list parameter is passed to the CPP in the format shown in Figure 3.13.

Figure 3.13 Compound List Parameter Example

0003	0036	0022	0008	0002	555555	666666	0002	333333	444444	0002	111111	222222
Number of Lists	Offset List 1	Offfset List 2	Offset List 3	List 3			List 2			List 1		

The CPP that processes this command is the CL program shown on the following page. For each list that the user specifies, the program must extract the *from* and *to account numbers*. First, it determines the number of lists that were entered by converting the first 2 bytes of the parameter string &ACCTLIST to the variable &LISTS.

Then, for each list, the CPP determines the offset value to use to find the list within the parameter string. The program then adds 3 to the offset value to accommodate two things. First, since the offset number actually positions you to the byte right before the start of the list, you must add one to the offset value to get to the first byte of the list. Also, since the first 2 bytes of a mixed list contain the binary value of the number of elements in the list (which we do not care about), we skip these 2 bytes by adding an additional two bytes to the offset value. This calculated offset value positions us to the **From account number** in each list. To find the **To account number**, we add 6 to our calculated offset value because the **From account number** occupies 6 bytes.

This routine is performed for each list the user specifies. The extracted *from* and *to account numbers* are then passed to the RPG program for processing.

```
            PGM          PARM(&WKREQ &ACCTLIST &WKOUTQ &WKCOPY)

/* DECLARE PROGRAM VARIABLES */
            DCL          VAR(&WKREQ) TYPE(*CHAR) LEN(10)
            DCL          VAR(&ACCTLIST) TYPE(*CHAR) LEN(72) /* List +
                           of Account Ranges */
            DCL          VAR(&WKOUTQ) TYPE(*CHAR) LEN(10)
            DCL          VAR(&WKCOPY) TYPE(*CHAR) LEN(2)

            DCL          VAR(&JOBTYPE) TYPE(*CHAR) LEN(1)
            DCL          VAR(&FRACCT1) TYPE(*CHAR) LEN(6)
            DCL          VAR(&TOACCT1) TYPE(*CHAR) LEN(6)
            DCL          VAR(&FRACCT2) TYPE(*CHAR) LEN(6)
            DCL          VAR(&TOACCT2) TYPE(*CHAR) LEN(6)
            DCL          VAR(&FRACCT3) TYPE(*CHAR) LEN(6)
            DCL          VAR(&TOACCT3) TYPE(*CHAR) LEN(6)
            DCL          VAR(&FRACCT4) TYPE(*CHAR) LEN(6)
            DCL          VAR(&TOACCT4) TYPE(*CHAR) LEN(6)
            DCL          VAR(&FRACCT5) TYPE(*CHAR) LEN(6)
            DCL          VAR(&TOACCT5) TYPE(*CHAR) LEN(6)
            DCL          VAR(&OFFSET) TYPE(*DEC) LEN(5 0)
            DCL          VAR(&LISTS) TYPE(*DEC) LEN(5 0)
            DCL          VAR(&BIN) TYPE(*CHAR) LEN(2)    /* BINARY VALUE */
            DCL          VAR(&DEC) TYPE(*DEC) LEN(5 0) /* DECIMAL VALUE */

/* DETERMINE IF JOB IS SUBMITTED VERSION OR INTERACTIVE VERSION */
            RTVJOBA      TYPE(&JOBTYPE)
            IF           COND(&JOBTYPE *EQ '1') THEN(DO)
            SBMJOB       CMD(CALL PGM(GLACCTCL) PARM(&WKREQ &ACCTLIST +
                           &WKOUTQ &WKCOPY)) JOB(GLACCT) JOBQ(QBATCH) +
                           HOLD(*YES)
            SNDPGMMSG    MSG('The G/L Account Report has been +
                           Submitted on Hold') MSGTYPE(*INFO)
            GOTO         CMDLBL(END)
            ENDDO

/* INITIALIZE PROGRAM VARIABLES WITH DATA */
/*    EXTRACT ACCT NUMBER RANGES */
            CHGVAR       &BIN %SST(&ACCTLIST 1 2) /*Extract # of LISTS */
            CHGVAR       &LISTS %BINARY(&BIN 1 2)

            IF           COND(&LISTS *GE 01) THEN(DO)
            CHGVAR       &BIN %SST(&ACCTLIST 3 2) /*Extract OFFSET 1 */
            CHGVAR       &OFFSET %BINARY(&BIN 1 2)
            CHGVAR       VAR(&OFFSET) VALUE(&OFFSET + 3)
            CHGVAR       VAR(&FRACCT1) VALUE(%SST(&ACCTLIST &OFFSET 6))
            CHGVAR       VAR(&OFFSET) VALUE(&OFFSET + 6)
            CHGVAR       VAR(&TOACCT1) VALUE (%SST(ACCTLIST &OFFSET 6))
            ENDDO

            IF           COND(&LISTS *GE 02) THEN(DO)
            CHGVAR       &BIN %SST(&ACCTLIST 5 2) /*Extract OFFSET 2 */
            CHGVAR       &OFFSET %BINARY(&BIN 1 2)
            CHGVAR       VAR(&OFFSET) VALUE(&OFFSET + 3)
            CHGVAR       VAR(&FRACCT2) VALUE(%SST(&ACCTLIST &OFFSET 6))
```

```
            CHGVAR      VAR(&OFFSET) VALUE(&OFFSET + 6)
            CHGVAR      VAR(&TOACCT2) VALUE(%SST(&ACCTLIST &OFFSET 6))
            ENDDO

            IF          COND(&LISTS *GE 03) THEN(DO)
            CHGVAR      &BIN %SST(&ACCTLIST 7 2) /*Extract OFFSET 3 */
            CHGVAR      &OFFSET %BINARY(&BIN 1 2)
            CHGVAR      VAR(&OFFSET) VALUE(&OFFSET + 3)
            CHGVAR      VAR(&FRACCT3) VALUE(%SST(&ACCTLIST &OFFSET 6))
            CHGVAR      VAR(&OFFSET) VALUE(&OFFSET + 6)
            CHGVAR      VAR(&TOACCT3) VALUE(%SST(&ACCTLIST &OFFSET 6))
            ENDDO

            IF          COND(&LISTS *GE 04) THEN(DO)
            CHGVAR      &BIN %SST(&ACCTLIST 9 2) /*Extract OFFSET 4 */
            CHGVAR      &OFFSET %BINARY(&BIN 1 2)

            CHGVAR      VAR(&OFFSET) VALUE(&OFFSET + 3)
            CHGVAR      VAR(&FRACCT4) VALUE(%SST(&ACCTLIST &OFFSET 6))
            CHGVAR      VAR(&OFFSET) VALUE(&OFFSET + 6)
            CHGVAR      VAR(&TOACCT4) VALUE(%SST(&ACCTLIST &OFFSET 6))
            ENDDO

            IF          COND(&LISTS *GE 05) THEN(DO)
            CHGVAR      &BIN %SST(&ACCTLIST 11 2) /*Extract OFFSET 5 */
            CHGVAR      &OFFSET %BINARY(&BIN 1 2)

            CHGVAR      VAR(&OFFSET) VALUE(&OFFSET + 3)
            CHGVAR      VAR(&FRACCT5) VALUE(%SST(&ACCTLIST &OFFSET 6))
            CHGVAR      VAR(&OFFSET) VALUE(&OFFSET + 6)
            CHGVAR      VAR(&TOACCT5) VALUE(%SST(&ACCTLIST &OFFSET 6))
            ENDDO
```

```
/* OVERRIDE PRINTER FILES */
            OVRPRTF     FILE(GLACCT) TOFILE(QSYSPRT) OUTQ(&WORKOUTQ) +
                          COPIES(&WKCOPY) USRDTA(&WKREQ)


/* CALL GL ACCT REPORT PROGRAM */
            CALL        PGM(GLACCT) PARM(&WKREQ &FRACCT1 &TOACCT1 +
                          &FRACCT2 &TOACCT2 &FRACCT3 &TOACCT3 +
                          &FRACCT4 &TOACCT4 &FRACCT5 &TOACCT5)

END:        ENDPGM
```

Qualified Parameters

Chapter 4

The QUAL statement provides the ability to qualify a parameter with additional values.

When prompting for parameters, you sometimes want the user to further qualify a parameter value. For example, when prompting for a file name, you usually have to determine the library for that file. The QUAL statement provides for this function. It lets you qualify a parameter with additional values.

Figure 4.1 shows the IBM WRKOUTQ (Work with Output Queue) command prompt screen. The first parameter, **Output queue**, is ·qualified by **Library**. This is an example of a qualified name. Notice how the qualifying parameter, **Library**, is indented beneath the qualified parameter, **Output queue**. This visual clue indicates to the user that the value for library is associated with the value for output queue. IBM-supplied commands use qualified names extensively.

Figure 4.1 WORKOUTQ Command Illustrating a Qualified Name

```
                        Work with Output Queue (WRKOUTQ)

 Type choices, press Enter.

 Output queue . . . . . . . . . . . . . .   *ALL           Name, *ALL
   Library. . . . . . . . . . . . . . .                    Name, *LIBL, *CURLIB
 Output . . . . . . . . . . . . . . . .   *                *, *PRINT

















                                                                        Bottom
 F3=Exit   F4=Prompt   F5=Refresh   F12=Cancel   F13=How to use this display
 F24=More keys
```

You will find uses for qualified parameters in your applications, too. The example in this chapter is a utility to create a duplicate spool file, which is useful when you need to have one report print on multiple printers in different physical locations.

Figure 4.2 DUPSPLF Command Prompt Screen Illustrating Qualified Names

```
                       DUPLICATE SPOOL FILE (DUPSPLF)

Type choices, press Enter.

SPOOL FILE NAME: . . . . . . . . . . . .        _____
JOB NAME OR * FOR CURRENT JOB:                  *
  USER NAME: . . . . . . . . . . . . .          _____
  JOB NUMBER: . . . . . . . . . . . .           _____
PRINTER FILE NAME: . . . . . . . . . .          QSYSPRT
  LIBRARY NAME:  . . . . . . . . . . .           *LIBL
SPOOLED OUTPUT QUEUE NAME: . . . . . . .        *PRTFILE
  LIBRARY NAME:  . . . . . . . . . . .           *LIBL
SPOOL FILE NBR OR *ONLY,*LAST: . . . . .        *ONLY




                                                           Bottom
F3=Exit   F4=Prompt   F5=Refresh   F12=Cancel   F13=How to use this display
F24=More keys
```

Coding the QUAL Statement

The example in Figure 4.2 uses three different qualified names. The first one, **Job Name**, is qualified by **User Name** and **Job Number**. The second one, **Printer File Name**, is qualified by **Library Name**. And the third qualified name, **Spooled Output Queue Name**, is qualified by **Library Name**. You use the QUAL statement to define qualified names. The following code shows the command source to create this prompt screen:

```
CMD       PROMPT('DUPLICATE SPOOL FILE')
PARM      KWD(FILE) TYPE(*NAME) LEN(10) MIN(1) +
          EXPR(*YES) PROMPT('SPOOL FILE NAME:')
PARM      KWD(JOB) TYPE(QUAL1) DFT(*) SNGVAL((*)) +
          PROMPT('JOB NAME OR * FOR CURRENT JOB:')
PARM      KWD(PRTFILE) TYPE(QUAL2) PROMPT('PRINTER +
          FILE NAME:')
PARM      KWD(OUTQ) TYPE(QUAL3) PROMPT('SPOOLED OUTPUT +
          QUEUE NAME:')
PARM      KWD(SPLNBR) TYPE(*CHAR) LEN(6) DFT(*ONLY) +
          RANGE(0001 9999) SPCVAL((*ONLY) (*LAST)) +
          PROMPT('SPOOL FILE NBR OR *ONLY,*LAST:')
QUAL1:    QUAL    TYPE(*NAME) LEN(10) MIN(1) EXPR(*YES)
```

```
           QUAL     TYPE(*NAME) LEN(10) MIN(0) EXPR(*YES) +
                      PROMPT('USER NAME:')
           QUAL     TYPE(*CHAR) LEN(6) RANGE(000000 999999) +
                      MIN(0) FULL(*YES) PROMPT('JOB NUMBER:')
QUAL2:     QUAL     TYPE(*NAME) LEN(10) DFT(QSYSPRT) EXPR(*YES)
           QUAL     TYPE(*NAME) LEN(10) DFT(*LIBL) +
                      SPCVAL((*LIBL)) EXPR(*YES) +
                      PROMPT('LIBRARY NAME:')
QUAL3:     QUAL     TYPE(*NAME) LEN(10) DFT(*PRTFILE) +
                      SPCVAL((*LIBL)) EXPR(*YES) =
           QUAL     TYPE(*NAME) LEN(10) DFT(*LIBL) +
                      SPCVAL((*LIBL)) EXPR(*YES) +
                      PROMPT('LIBRARY NAME:')
```

Define qualifying fields in a QUAL statement, not in a PARM statement.

Look at the bottom of the command source member above, and notice the QUAL statements. Each input field that is part of a qualified name has one QUAL statement. The QUAL statements are uniquely labeled for each qualified name, and each label is referenced in a PARM statement. Notice that each qualified name group has only one PARM statement. You define the qualifying fields only in a QUAL statement — you do not code a PARM statement for them.

Let's look at the qualified group of fields for **Job Name**. You code the qualified field, JOB, with a PARM statement that specifies a TYPE of QUAL1. This is not really a TYPE, but simply a label, referencing the group of QUAL statements associated with the label QUAL1: at the bottom of the command source member. (Figure 4.3 illustrates this association of the TYPE keyword with the label. This coding method works just like the ELEM statement does when you define a mixed list.

Figure 4.3 Coding Qualified Fields

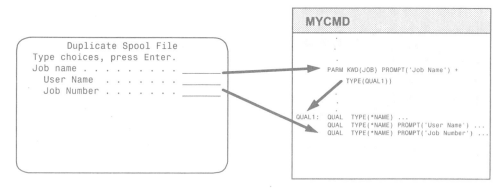

QUAL statements, not PARM statements, define the fields for the qualified names. The QUAL statement is very similar to the PARM statement and shares many of the same keywords, such as TYPE, LEN,

PROMPT, MIN, RANGE. (see Appendix B for an extensive list of QUAL keywords).

The first QUAL statement in a group further defines the qualified parameter; QUAL statements for qualifying parameters follow in the group.

The first QUAL statement of a group always defines the qualified parameter (the first parameter in the group), and the following QUAL statements are the qualifying parameters (the remaining parameters in the group). In the example, the qualified parameter, PRTFILE, is the first QUAL statement in the group labeled QUAL2. The QUAL statement below it defines the qualifying parameter, **Library Name**. A group will always have at least two QUAL statements: one qualified value and at least one qualifying value. Notice that the first QUAL statement does not have a PROMPT value since this is already specified on the PARM statement.

The first QUAL statement of a qualified name must have as the TYPE either *NAME or *GENERIC. Although this might seem like a strange restriction, it makes sense when you think in terms of IBM's use of commands to qualify names of system objects such as files or devices.

You can qualify not only regular parameters, but also parameters in a list (simple, mixed, or compound). You can use separate PARMs instead of qualified names, but a qualified name improves the readability of the screen by showing the user that the parameters are related.

Processing Qualified Parameters

The values of a qualified parameter are passed to the CPP as a single parameter, in the order they appear in the command source.

As you might have guessed, the processing of qualified and qualifying parameters requires special code in the CPP. The values of a qualified name are passed to the CPP as one single parameter. For example, a qualified name, consisting of a 10-character file name and a 10-character library name, is passed as one 20-character value. Within that single parameter, the values appear in the order in which you defined them in the source.

Use CL's %SST substring parameter to extract individual values from a qualified parameter.

The following code sample shows a section of the CL program that is the CPP for command DUPSPLF, shown in Figure 4.2. We will concentrate on the sections of code that process the qualified name for the job name parameter. We use the substring built-in function to extract the individual values into separate variables.

```
PGM         PARM(&FILE &FULLJOB &PRTFILE &OUTQ &SPLNBR)
/*DEFINE JOB NAME VARIABLES */
            DCL         VAR(&FULLJOB) TYPE(*CHAR) LEN(26)
            DCL         VAR(&JOB) TYPE(*CHAR) LEN(10)
            DCL         VAR(&USER) TYPE(*CHAR) LEN(10)
            DCL         VAR(&JOBNBR) TYPE(*CHAR) LEN(6)
                              .
                              .
                              .
                              .
```

```
/* EXTRACT JOB VARIABLES */
           CHGVAR      VAR(&JOB) VALUE(%SST(&FULLJOB 1 10))
           CHGVAR      VAR(&USER) VALUE(%SST(&FULLJOB 11 10))
           CHGVAR      VAR(&JOBNBR) VALUE(%SST(&FULLJOB 21 6))
```

We begin the program by defining the parameters in the PGM command. Notice that the job parameter (&FULLJOB) is specified as a single parameter. That is the way the command will pass it to the CPP. The variable, &FULLJOB, is 26 characters long because it contains the 10-character job name, the 10-character user name, and the 6-character job number (see Figure 4.4). The CHGVAR command extracts the individual parameters into their own variables. For example, the value of the variable &JOBNBR (job number) is extracted from the variable &FULLJOB, beginning in position 21, for 6 bytes. You need to include similar routines for each qualified parameter in the command.

Figure 4.4 Layout of Qualified Name Parameter

XXXXXXXXXX	XXXXXXXXXX	XXXXXX
&JOB	&USER	&JOBNBR

Conditional Prompting

Chapter 5

Conditional prompting determines which parameters are displayed on a prompt screen and when they are displayed. The two types of conditional prompting are additional parameters (conditioned by F10) and parameters conditioned on the value of other parameters (using PMTCTL).

Additional Parameters

Use conditional prompting for infrequently used optional parameters.

The first type of conditional prompting will be familiar to you. IBM uses F10 (additional parameters) in many of its commands. Parameters conditioned by the user pressing F10 are useful when parameters are optional and not frequently used. Figure 5.1 shows an IBM example.

Figure 5.1 CHGJOB Command Prompt Screen

```
                          Change Job (CHGJOB)

 Type choices, press Enter.

 Job name . . . . . . . . . . .   *_____      Name, *
   User . . . . . . . . . . . .   _____       Name
   Number . . . . . . . . . . .   _____       000000-999999












                                                              Bottom
 F3=Exit  F4=Prompt  F5=Refresh  F10=Additional parameters  F12=Cancel
 F13=How to use this display     F24=More keys
```

This command, CHGJOB, specifies **F10=Additional parameters**. After pressing F10, you will see the prompt shown in Figure 5.2 with the additional parameters.

Figure 5.2 CHGJOB Command Illustrating Additional Parameters Function

```
                             Change Job (CHGJOB)

 Type choices, press Enter.

 Job name . . . . . . . . . . .   *             Name, *
 User . . . . . . . . . . . . .                 Name
 Number . . . . . . . . . . . .                 000000-999999
 Job priority (on JOBQ) . . . .   *SAME         0-9, *SAME
 Output priority (on OUTQ). . . .  5            1-9, *SAME
 Print device . . . . . . . .     W27           Name, *SAME, *USRPRF...
 Output queue . . . . . . . .     NOPRINT       Name, *SAME, *USRPRF, *DEV...
 Library. . . . . . . . . . .     QGPL          Name, *LIBL, *CURLIB
 Run priority . . . . . . . .     20            1-99, *SAME

                           Additional Parameters
 Job queue. . . . . . . . . .     *SAME         Name, *SAME
 Library. . . . . . . . . . .                   Name, *LIBL, *CURLIB
 Print text . . . . . . . . .     *BLANK

                                                                    More...
 F3=Exit   F4=Prompt   F5=Refresh   F12=Cancel   F13=How to use this display
 F24=More keys
```

Like many of the other functions in commands, specifying some of the parameters as "additional" and using F10 to condition the display are easy tasks. To condition parameters on F10, you simply use the PMTCTL keyword with a value of *PMTRQS (Prompt Request) on the PARM to be conditioned.

Application Example

In the command shown in Figure 5.3, users will usually have to enter only the quotation number and the sort sequence for the quote comparison they want to run. The prompt screen with the minimum information is what they initially see.

Figure 5.3 Command Using Additional Parameters Function

```
                     ·Quote Comparison - Internal (SA311CMD)

 Type choices, press Enter.

 Quotation Number. . . . . . .    _____        Value, or F4 for list
 Sort Sequence . . . . . . . . .                S=Seq B=Base C=Compar D=Desc
 Compare Cost To . . . . . . . .   B            B=Base, C=Comparison
 Requester . . . . . . . . . .
 Printer Output Queue. . . . . .   QPRINT____    Value, or F4 for list
 Number of Copies . . . . . . .    01            01-99





                                                                    Bottom
 F3=Exit   F4=Prompt   F5=Refresh   F10=Additional parameters   F12=Cancel
 F13=How to use this display        F24=More keys
```

As you can see in Figure 5.3, when users need to run a quote comparison for a specific costing warehouse, they will press F10 to display the additional field, as shown in Figure 5.4.

Figure 5.4 Command Showing Additional Parameters

```
                      Quote Comparison - Internal (SA311CMD)

  Type choices, press Enter.

  Quotation Number . . . . . . . .    _____        Value, or F4 for list
  Sort Sequence. . . . . . . . . .                  S=Seq B=Base C=Compar D=Desc
  Compare Cost To. . . . . . . . .    B             B=Base, C=Comparison
  Requester. . . . . . . . . . .
  Printer Output Queue . . . . . .    QPRINT____    Value, or F4 for list
  Number of Copies . . . . . . . .    01            01-99

  Additional Parameters
  Costing Warehouse . . . . . . . .   80_           Value, or F4 for list





                                                                     Bottom
  F3=Exit   F4=Prompt   F5=Refresh   F12=Cancel   F13=How to use this display
  F24=More keys
```

Coding the PMTCTL Command

The source member for the PMTCTL command, shown below, uses the PMTCTL keyword of the PARM statement to enable the use of F10. The sixth PARM (WH) specifies PMTCTL(*PMTRQS), indicating that this value is to be displayed only when F10 is used.

```
CMD           PROMPT('Quote Comparison - Internal')
PARM          KWD(QUOTE) TYPE(*DEC) LEN(6) RANGE(000001 +
                999999) MIN(1) CHOICE(*PGM) +
                CHOICEPGM(CHCQUOTE) PROMPT('Quotation +
                Number' 1)
PARM          KWD(SORT) TYPE(*CHAR) LEN(1) RSTD(*YES) +
                VALUES(S B C D) MIN(1) CHOICE('S=Seq +
                B=Base C=Compar D=Desc') PROMPT('Sort +
                Sequence' 2)
PARM          KWD(REQUESTER) TYPE(*CHAR) LEN(10) MIN(1) +
                CHOICE(*NONE) PROMPT('Requester')
PARM          KWD(OUTQ) TYPE(*NAME) DFT(QPRINT) +
                CHOICE(*PGM) CHOICEPGM(CHCOUTQ) +
                PROMPT('Printer Output Queue')
PARM          KWD(COPIES) TYPE(*CHAR) LEN(2) DFT(01) +
                RANGE(01 99) PROMPT('Number of Copies')
PARM          KWD(WH) TYPE(*CHAR) LEN(3) DFT(80) +
                CHOICE(*PGM) CHOICEPGM(CHCWH) +
                PMTCTL(*PMTRQS) PROMPT('Costing Warehouse')
PARM          KWD(SOURCE) TYPE(*CHAR) LEN(1) CONSTANT(' ')
PARM          KWD(ATTN) TYPE(*CHAR) LEN(25) CONSTANT(' ')
PARM          KWD(CMT) TYPE(*CHAR) LEN(50) CONSTANT(' ')
PARM          KWD(COSTFLAG) TYPE(*CHAR) LEN(1) RSTD(*YES) +
                DFT(B) VALUES(B C) CHOICE('B=Base, +
                C=Comparison') PROMPT('Compare Cost To' 3)
```

You will see a few new keywords in this example, but ignore them for now. The PMTCTL(*PMTRQS) keyword on the costing warehouse PARM statement is the only keyword that is related to creating the prompt screen with a field that is hidden until F10 is pressed. This one keyword sets the field up as conditional, adds F10 to the function key list, and adds logic to display the field when the user presses F10.

Conditioning Other Parameters

Use conditional prompting when the display of one parameter depends upon the value of another parameter.

You can also use conditional prompting when the prompting of one parameter depends upon the value of another parameter. For example, the IBM DSPDBR command, shown in Figure 5.5, prompts the user for the value of the PARM, Output. If the user enters *OUTFILE in the parameter, additional parameters appear, as shown in Figure 5.6. These additional parameters are necessary to determine the information about the output file, such as file name and library.

Figure 5.5 DSPDBR Command, Using Conditional Prompting

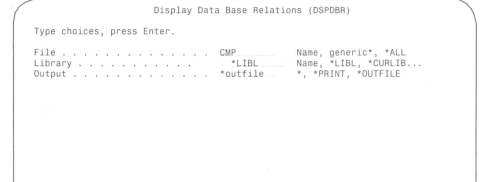

```
                     Display Data Base Relations (DSPDBR)

Type choices, press Enter.

File . . . . . . . . . . . . . .   CMP          Name, generic*, *ALL
Library . . . . . . . . . . . .        *LIBL    Name, *LIBL, *CURLIB...
Output . . . . . . . . . . . .     *outfile     *, *PRINT, *OUTFILE








                                                                  Bottom
 F3=Exit  F4=Prompt  F5=Refresh  F10=Additional parameters  F12=Cancel
```

Figure 5.6 DSPDBR Command, Using Conditional Prompting, Additional Parameters

```
                     Display Data Base Relations (DSPDBR)

Type choices, press Enter.

File . . . . . . . . . . . . .   CMP          Name, generic*, *ALL
   Library. . . . . . . . . . .       *LIBL    Name, *LIBL, *CURLIB...
   Output . . . . . . . . . . .     *OUTFILE   *, *PRINT, *OUTFILE
File to receive output . . . .                Name
   Library . . . . . . . . . . .       *LIBL   Name, *LIBL, *CURLIB
Output member options:
   Member to receive output . . .  *FIRST      Name, *FIRST
   Replace or add records . . . .  *REPLACE    *REPLACE, *ADD




                                                                  Bottom
 F3=Exit    F4=Prompt   F5=Refresh   F12=Cancel   F13=How to use this display
 F24=More keys
```

In this example, the presentation of the conditioned parameters (**File to receive output** and **Output member options**) depends on the value of the controlling parameter, **Output** (if the value is *OUTFILE). If the user enters * instead of *OUTFILE, the **Output Member Options** parameters are not displayed.

Just as a little review, this example also uses both qualified names and a mixed list. The qualified names are **File** and **File To Receive Output** (both qualified by the parameters **Library**). The mixed list is the **Output Member Options** parameter because it contains two separately defined elements.

Application Example

You will also find applications for this type of parameter conditioning in the commands you write. Figure 5.7 shows an application command using this type of conditional prompting. This command prompts the user for information to identify source members to scan for the SBMJOB command. This utility loads submitted program names into a PGMREF file to use in later analysis of cross-referenced programs.

Figure 5.7 FNDSBM Command, Using Conditional Prompting

```
                          Find SBMJOB (FNDSBM)

 Type choices, press Enter.

 Source Member Name . . . . . . .  *ALL          Name, *ALL
 CL File Name . . . . . . . . . .     QCLSRC     Name
 Library Name . . . . . . . . . .                Name
 Update PGMREF File?. . . . . . .  Y             Y, N












                                                            Bottom
 F3=Exit   F4=Prompt   F5=Refresh   F12=Cancel   F13=How to use this display
 F24=More keys
```

One of the options of the command is to update the PGMREF file when a match is found. If the user specifies **Y** to update the PGMREF file, the command prompt for the PGMREF file name and library, as shown in Figure 5.8.

Figure 5.8 FNDSBM Command, Displaying Conditioned Parameters

```
                          Find SBMJOB (FNDSBM)

 Type choices, press Enter.

 Source Member Name . . . . . . .   *ALL_____    Name, *ALL
   CL File Name . . . . . . . . .    QCLSRC_____    Name
   Library Name . . . . . . . . .    _____    Name
 Update PGMREF File?. . . . . . .   Y              Y, N
 PGMREF File Name . . . . . . . .    _____    Name
   PGMREF Library Name. . . . . .    _____    Name




                                                              Bottom
 F3=Exit    F4=Prompt    F5=Refresh    F12=Cancel    F13=How to use this display
 F24=More keys
```

The presentation of the prompt for the file name and library parameters is conditioned on the value of the **Update PGMREF File** parameter. To condition the presentation of one parameter on the value of another, you must have a controlling parameter and a conditioned parameter. The parameter **Update PGMREF File** is the controlling parameter. The parameter **PGMREF File Name** is the conditioned parameter. Here, the conditioned parameter is displayed only when the value of the controlling parameter is **Y**.

Coding the PMTCTL Command

Use PARM statements to define both controlling and conditioned parameters; for conditioned parameters, use the PMTCTL keyword to link the parameter to a condition.

A PARM statement defines the controlling parameter. PARM statements also define the conditioned parameters, but the conditioned parameters use the PMTCTL keyword of the PARM statement with the PMTCTL command definition statement (the PMTCTL statement is the fifth of the six command definition statements we are covering). The following command source code will make this concept clearer:

```
             CMD       PROMPT('Find SBMJOB')
             PARM      KWD(MBR) TYPE(QUAL1) PROMPT('Source Member +
                         Name')
             PARM      KWD(UPDREF) TYPE(*CHAR) LEN(1) RSTD(*YES) +
                         DFT(N) VALUES(Y N) PROMPT('Update PGMREF +
                         File?')
             PARM      KWD(REFILE) TYPE(QUAL2) PMTCTL(CONDITION1) +
                         PROMPT('PGMREF File Name')
 QUAL1:      QUAL      TYPE(*NAME) LEN(10) DFT(*ALL) SPCVAL((*ALL))
```

```
                  QUAL       TYPE(*NAME) LEN(10) DFT(QCLSRC) PROMPT('CL +
                             File Name')
                  QUAL       TYPE(*NAME) LEN(10) PROMPT('Library Name')
    QUAL2:        QUAL       TYPE(*NAME) LEN(10)
                  QUAL       TYPE(*NAME) LEN(10) PROMPT('PGMREF Library +
                             Name')
   CONDITION1: PMTCTL        CTL(UPDREF) COND((*EQ Y))
```

The above code is the source member for the FNDSBM command and illustrates how to define conditional prompting. As usual, a PARM statement defines the controlling parameter, UPDREF. The conditioned parameter, REFILE, is also defined on a PARM statement (which happens to be a qualified name). To define the relationship between UPDREF and REFILE, we use the PMTCTL keyword to reference a label, CONDITION1. This label is used on the associated PMTCTL statement. The PMTCTL statement controls when to display the conditioned parameter; for example, when UPDREF is equal to **Y**.

The PARM statement's PMTCTL keyword links a conditioned parameter to a separate PMTCTL statement, which defines the condition.

Don't confuse the PMTCTL *command definition statement* with the PMTCTL *keyword* of the PARM statement. The PMTCTL keyword of the PARM statement determines what PMTCTL statement the PARM is conditioned on. The PMTCTL command definition statement defines the conditions to test.

PMTCTL Keywords

The PMTCTL command definition statement has four keywords of its own. They are CTL (controlling parameter), COND (condition), NBRTRUE (number true), and LGLREL (logical relationship). This example uses the first two, CTL and COND.

The CTL keyword of the PMTCTL statement simply references the PARM (by keyword name) that is the controlling parameter for the condition. In this example, UPDREF is the controlling parameter because its value is to be tested.

The COND keyword of the PMTCTL statement specifies the conditions to test. In this example, the controlling parameter must equal **Y**. If this condition is met, the parameter(s) referencing this PMTCTL statement (REFILE) will be displayed.

The PMTCTL command statement is very flexible. It lets you test many combinations of conditions. You can test a single controlling parameter for multiple conditions. The additional conditions are simply included in the COND keyword. For example, if the presentation of a parameter for OUTQ is based on the value of the output type being *PRINT or *ALL, you use the following PARM and PMTCTL statements:

```
          PARM       KWD(OUTTYPE) TYPE(*CHAR) LEN(6) RSTD(*YES) +
                       VALUES(* *PRINT *ALL) MIN(1) PROMPT('Output Type')
          PARM       KWD(OUTQ) TYPE(*NAME) DFT(QPRINT) PMTCTL(COND) +
                       PROMPT('Output Queue')
COND:     PMTCTL     CTL(OUTTYPE) COND((*EQ *PRINT) (*EQ *ALL)) +
                       NBRTRUE(*EQ 1)
```

The NBRTRUE keyword indicates how many of the conditions must be true. In this case, only one of the conditions must be true for the PARM using this PMTCTL statement to be displayed. If NBRTRUE is 2, both conditions have to be met (physically impossible in this example). The NBRTRUE keyword lets you define AND/OR conditions. NBRTRUE(1) represents an OR condition, while NBRTRUE(2) represents an AND condition. You can specify up to 50 conditions in a single PMTCTL statement.

You also can condition the conditioned parameter on more than one controlling parameter. Simply use additional PMTCTL statements (all grouped under the same label). For example, if the presentation of a parameter is based on the GENDER being M and the AGE being greater than or equal to 18, the following PMTCTL statements are used:

```
          PARM       KWD(GENDER) TYPE(*CHAR) LEN(1) RSTD(*YES) +
                       DFT(M) VALUES(M F) PROMPT('Gender')
          PARM       KWD(AGE) TYPE(*DEC) LEN(3 0) RANGE(0 150) +
                       PROMPT('Age')
          PARM       KWD(SHAVES) TYPE(*CHAR) LEN(1) RSTD(*YES) +
                       VALUES(Y N) PMTCTL(COND) PROMPT('Shaves?')
COND:     PMTCTL     CTL(GENDER) COND((*EQ M))
          PMTCTL     CTL(AGE) COND((*GE 18)) LGLREL(*AND)
```

The additional PMTCTL statements may use the LGLREL keyword (logical relationship) to determine whether the relationship between PMTCTL statements is *AND or *OR (the default is *AND). Using the NBRTRUE and LGLREL keywords will let you create any variety of conditions you will need for your applications.

Dependent Relationships

Chapter 6

The DEP statement allows conditional checking for a dependent relationship between parameters.

Applications that prompt users for parameters sometimes need to enforce a specific relationship between parameters. For example, if you request a date range by prompting for a start date and an end date, you are wise to make sure that the start date is less than or equal to the end date or that the end date is greater than or equal to the start date. That is a dependent relationship, because the value of one parameter depends on the value of another parameter. To define a dependent relationship, you use the DEP statement, the last of the six command definition statements.

We have already seen a similar function that the REL (relationship) keyword of the PARM statement provides. The DEP statement performs the same type of dependency checking that the PARM statement provides, but DEP offers much more power and flexibility. The most significant difference between the two statements is that the DEP statement allows the checking of the specified relationship to be conditional. The DEP statement is a very powerful command definition statement. It allows a form of data editing by enforcing specified relationships among command parameters.

Application Example

The example in Figure 6.1 shows a prompt screen for the TAATAPC command from QUSRTOOL that copies a distribution tape. The screen prompts for a **From device** and a **To device**. Because these two devices cannot logically be the same, you must ensure that they contain two different values. This example uses the DEP statement to enforce that dependent relationship. When you enter the same value for both parameters (not meeting the required relationship), a message appears that states, "Requirements between parameters not satisfied." This is not very descriptive, but you can customize the message; we will discuss how to do that shortly.

Figure 6.1 Command TAATAPC Prompt Screen

```
                      Copy Distribution Tape (TAATAPC)

Type choices, press Enter.

From device . . . . . . . . . . . . .   TAP01_____   Name
To device . . . . . . . . . . . . .     TAP01_____   Name
To sequence number. . . . . . . . .     1_____     Number, *END
TODEV end of tape file option . . . .   *REWIND___   *LEAVE, *REWIND, *UNLOAD
Licensed programs to copy . . . . . .   *PROMPT___   *PROMPT, *ALL, 5738AAA-5728999
                 + for more values




                                                                    Bottom
F3=Exit    F4=Prompt    F5=Refresh    F121=Cancel    F13=How to use this display
F24-More keys
Requirements between parameters not satisfied.
```

DEP Keywords

The command source for the TAATAPC command is shown in the code
that follows. You define the two parameters having the required
relationship in the same way as you define any other parameter: with the
PARM statement. The relationship between the parameters is defined in
the DEP statement, shown at the bottom of the command.

```
CMD         PROMPT('Copy Distribution Tape')
PARM        KWD(FROMDEV) TYPE(*NAME) LEN(10) +
              MIN(1) EXPR(*YES) PROMPT('From device')
PARM        KWD(TODEV) TYPE(*NAME) LEN(10) +
              MIN(1) EXPR(*YES) PROMPT('To device')
PARM        KWD(TOSEQNBR) TYPE(*DEC) LEN(4 0) DFT(1) +
              SPCVAL((*END 0)) +
              PROMPT('To sequence number')
PARM        KWD(ENDOPT) TYPE(*CHAR) LEN(7) DFT(*REWIND) +
              RSTD(*YES) VALUES('*LEAVE' '*REWIND' +
              '*UNLOAD') +
              PROMPT('TODEV end of tape file option')
PARM        KWD(LICPGM) TYPE(*CHAR) LEN(7) +
              DFT(*PROMPT) RANGE('5738AAA' '5799999') +
              SNGVAL((*ALL)(*PROMPT)) MIN(0) MAX(200) +
              ALWUNPRT(*NO) FULL(*YES) EXPR(*YES) +
              CHOICE('*PROMPT, *ALL, 5738AAA-5728999') +
              PROMPT('Licensed programs to copy')
DEP         CTL(*ALWAYS) PARM((&FROMDEV *NE &TODEV)) +
              NBRTRUE(*EQ 1)
```

The DEP statement uses some very awkward syntax, so let's make it simple. The DEP statement has three basic keywords that perform three different functions. They are

- PARM — the relationship(s) to be tested
- CTL — the condition(s) controlling when to test the relationship(s)
- NBRTRUE — the number of relationships that must be true to satisfy the dependency

Although keywords for the DEP statement have the same names as the keywords for the PMTCTL statement, they are not all used the same way. For example, the CTL keyword for the PMTCTL statement indicates the controlling parameter for a condition, while the CTL keyword for the DEP statement specifies the controlling conditions.

The PARM keyword of the DEP command definition statement describes the actual relationship(s) to be tested. This example tests the value of the parameter FROMDEV against the value of the parameter TODEV. The relationship to be tested is *EQ (equal). The two parameters will be checked to determine whether they are equal to each other.

The CTL keyword of the DEP statement defines the controlling conditions under which to perform the testing of the relationship. In the example, the condition is *ALWAYS, which means that the dependency is always checked.

The NBRTRUE keyword of the DEP command definition statement determines the number of relationships that must be true to satisfy the dependency. For example, when NBRTRUE is equal to 1, the two parameters should never be equal to each other.

Our example DEP statement indicates that, in all cases, FROMDEV should not be equal to TODEV. This awkwardness of expression makes the DEP statement difficult to comprehend at first, but after reviewing several examples, you will find it becoming clearer.

Defining Relationships

The PARM keyword of the DEP statement can define relationships in several ways. You can define up to 25 relationships in one DEP statement. Within a relationship, you can compare the value of a parameter keyword not only to that of another parameter keyword (as in the last example), but also to a specific value. The example that follows shows multiple relationships and compares a PARM to a value:

```
DEP    CTL(*ALWAYS) PARM((&FILE *NE *ALL) +
       (&LIB *NE *ALL) NBRTRUE(*EQ 1)
```

This DEP statement ensures that the &FILE parameter and the &LIB parameter cannot both be *ALL. Either one may be *ALL, but not both of them at the same time.

The PARM keyword of the DEP statement can also check for the presence of a value in a specified parameter keyword. In this case, the PARM parameter contains only the name of the parameter keyword to be checked. For example, look at the following code:

```
DEP    CTL(*ALWAYS) PARM(FLAG)
```

The DEP statement ensures that the PARM, FLAG, is entered. In other words, the DEP statement makes the FLAG PARM mandatory. This is a special use of the PARM keyword and this use has a special rule. When checking for the presence of a value in a parameter keyword, you must specify the keyword in the PARM parameter without a leading &. This rule applies only when you are checking for the presence of a value in a parameter keyword. All other uses of the keyword within the PARM keyword in the DEP statement will require the leading & to identify the value as a parameter name.

Defining Conditions

The CTL keyword of the DEP statement can be very useful. This keyword is what sets the DEP statement apart from the REL keyword of the PARM statement. You use the default value, *ALWAYS, when a dependent relationship is unconditional and should always be checked. The real power of the CTL keyword is in its ability to specify special conditions under which the dependency should be checked. For example, look at the following code:

```
DEP    CTL(&OBJTYPE *EQ PGM) PARM(&COPYDATA *NE YES)
```

This DEP statement will not allow the &COPYDATA parameter to be YES if the &OBJTYPE parameter is PGM. Both &OBJTYPE and &COPYDATA must be parameters that have been defined in the command with PARM statements.

The conditions the CTL keyword defines can compare the value of a parameter keyword to a specific value (as in the prior example), or it can compare the value of a parameter keyword to the value of another parameter keyword. In addition, you can use the presence of a value in a parameter keyword as a condition, as in the following example:

```
EP     CTL(FILE) PARM(LIB)
```

This DEP statement says that if a value is in the FILE parameter, a value must be in the LIB parameter. Notice again that when you use the presence of a value in a parameter keyword as a condition, you specify the keyword without a leading &:

```
EP          CTL(USRPRF) PARM(&USRPRF *NE QSECOFR)
```

This example states that if a value is in the USRPRF parameter, this value cannot be QSECOFR.

Message Text

A fourth keyword of the DEP command definition statement is the MSGID keyword. You use this keyword to specify a message number from a message file that will be used to retrieve the message text that will appear when the dependent relationship is not met. A message file allows more specific detail in the message text. (Using message files is covered in detail in Chapter 7, "Message Files.")

Section 2

Command Tips and Techniques

Message Files

You can store the text for some command statement keywords in a message file.

Many of the command-definition-statement keywords allow entry of some sort of text. For example, on the PARM statement, the PROMPT keyword is where you specify the prompt text (the text that appears to the left of the input field). Many of these text keywords allow the use of a message file to store the text. Establishing frequently used text in a message file offers a simple method to provide consistent prompting. Figure 7.1 summarizes the keywords that allow message files for text.

Figure 7.1 Command Statements Using Message File for Text

Uses for Message Files in Commands	
Command Statement	**Keywords**
CMD	PROMPT
PARM	PROMPT, CHOICE
ELEM	PROMPT, CHOICE
QUAL	PROMPT, CHOICE
DEP	MSGID

The sample code that follows represents command source code that uses message files for the PROMPT text values. The PROMPT keywords of the PARM statements specify the message identifier that contains the prompt text. For example, the WKOUTQ PARM uses a message identifier (SAP0005) to store its text. This command prompts for the information required to run a report. The prompt text for these parameters is used frequently in other commands, so the text is stored in a message file.

```
CMD       PROMPT(SAP0001)
PARM      KWD(WKMMYY) TYPE(*CHAR) LEN(4) RANGE(0100 +
          1299) MIN(1) FULL(*YES) CHOICE(MMYY) +
          PROMPT(SAP0002)
PARM      KWD(WKREQ) TYPE(*CHAR) LEN(10) MIN(1) +
          CHOICE(*NONE) PROMPT(SAP0003)
```

```
PARM          KWD(WKOUTQ) TYPE(*CHAR) LEN(10) DFT(QPRINT) +
              CHOICE(*NONE) PROMPT(SAP0005)
PARM          KWD(WKCOPY) TYPE(*CHAR) LEN(2) DFT(1) MIN(0) +
              CHOICE(*NONE) PROMPT(SAP0004)
```

Creating a Message File

To create a message file, use the CRTMSGF (Create Message File) command, as shown in Figure 7.2. You may want to create a separate message file for each application.

Figure 7.2 Creating a Message File

```
                    Create Message File (CRTMSGF)

 Type choices, press Enter.

 Message file . . . . . . . . .   SAMSG        Name
   Library. . . . . . . . . .    *CURLIB      Name, *CURLIB
 Text 'description' . . . . . .   SALES ANALYSIS COMMAND MESSAGES




                                                            Bottom
 F3=Exit   F4=Prompt   F5=Refresh   F10=Additional Parameters   F12=Cancel
 F13=How to use this display       F24=More keys
```

You create the message file without any messages, much like you create a physical file without any data. After you have created the message file, you will add the message descriptions (the text) by using the ADDMSGD (Add Message Description) command. You need to specify only the message identifier and the first-level text on the command's prompt screen (Figure 7.3).

Figure 7.3 Message File Message Example

```
                        Add Message Description (ADDMSGD)

 Type choices, press Enter.

 Message identifier . . . . . . . .    SAP0005       Name
 Message file . . . . . . . . . . .    SAMSG         Name
 Library. . . . . . . . . . . . . .    *CURLIB       Name, *LIBL, *CURLIB
 First-level message text . . . . .    Printer Output Queue
 _____
 _____
 Second-level message text. . . . .    *NONE
 _____
 _____
 _____
 _____
 _____
                                                                       . . .
 Severity code. . . . . . . . . . .    00            0-99


                                                                      More...
 F3=Exit    F4=Prompt    F5=Refresh    F10=Additional parameters    F12=Cancel
 F13=How to use this display          F24=More keys
```

Our example message file (SAMSG) has the following five messages in it:

```
SAP0001   Monthly Sales Report
SAP0002   Fiscal Period
SAP0003   Requester
SAP0004   Number of Copies
SAP0005   Printer Output Queue
```

You can now use these messages in your command by referencing their message identifiers in the appropriate parameters, as shown in the code on pages 65 and 66.

The last step in using message files for prompt text involves creating the command object. When you compile the command, you must specify the appropriate message file name for the **Message file for prompt text** parameter, as shown in Figure 7.4.

Figure 7.4 CRTCMD Specifying Message Files

```
                        Create Command (CRTCMD)

 Type choices, press Enter.

 Where allowed to run. . . . . .   *ALL          *ALL, *BATCH, *INTERACT...
                + for more values
 Allow limited users . . . . . .   *NO           *NO, *YES
 Maximum positional parameters .   *NOMAX        0-75, *NOMAX
 Message file for prompt text. .   SAMSG         Name, *NONE
   Library . . . . . . . . . .       *CURLIB     Name, *LIBL, *CURLIB
 Message file. . . . . . . . . .   QCPFMSG       Name
   Library . . . . . . . . . .       *LIBL       Name, *LIBL, *CUR
 Help panel group. . . . . . . .   *NONE         Name, *NONE
   Library . . . . . . . . . .                   Name, *LIBL, *CURLIB
 Help identifier . . . . . . . .   *NONE         Character value, *CMD, *NONE
 Help search index . . . . . . .   *NONE         Name, *NONE, *SYSTEM
   Library . . . . . . . . . .                   Name, *LIBL, *CURLIB
 Current library . . . . . . . .   *NOCHG        Name, *NOCHG, *CRTDFT
 Product library . . . . . . . .   *NOCHG        Name, *NOCHG, *NONE


                                                                   More...
 F3=Exit   F4=Prompt   F5=Refresh   F12=Cancel   F13=How to use this display
 F24=More keys
```

Now, when the user executes this command, the system dynamically retrieves the prompt text from message file SAMSG, as shown in Figure 7.5.

Figure 7.5 Prompt Screen Using Message Files

```
                      Monthly Sales Report (SARPTCMD)

   Type choices, press Enter.

   Fiscal Period . . . . . . . . .                  MMYY
   Requester . . . . . . . . . . .
   Printer Output Queue. . . . . .   QPRINT
   Number of Copies. . . . . . . .   1












                                                                   Bottom
   F3=Exit   F4=Prompt   F5=Refresh   F12=Cancel   F13=How to use this display
   F24=More keys
```

Message Files with PROMPT

Message files allow you to support several languages with the same application programs and commands.

Message files provide great functionality in an international, multilingual environment. If one application must support several national languages, the use of message files lets you present a single command in several languages, with the message files supplying the prompt and choice text. You need only one program for all locations. A special library for each language stores the message files, so it is a simple matter of putting the appropriate message file library in the library list. For example, the library containing the French messages is in the French-speaking user's library list.

The following sample code represents the command source code for a simple prompt screen. The message identifiers for these parameters exist in three different libraries, one for English, one for French, and one for German. This single command can support all three.

```
CMD        PROMPT(SAP0001)
PARM       KWD(WKREQ) TYPE(*CHAR) LEN(10) MIN(1) +
             CHOICE(SAC001) PROMPT(SAP0003)
PARM       KWD(WKOUTQ) TYPE(*CHAR) LEN(10) DFT(QPRINT) +
             CHOICE(*NONE) PROMPT(SAP0005)
PARM       KWD(WKCOPY) TYPE(*CHAR) LEN(2) DFT(1)
             RANGE(01 99) PROMPT(SAP0004)
```

The English messages are shown in Figure 7.6, the German messages are shown in Figure 7.7, and the French messages are shown in Figure 7.8.

Figure 7.6 English Message File

```
                    Work with Message Descriptions
                                                   System: S1029115
   Message file:   SAMSG        Library: ENGLIB

   Position to . . . . . . .  _____     Message ID

   Type options, press Enter.
     2=Change   4=Delete   5=Display details   6=Print

   Opt  Message ID  Severity   Message Text
   _    SAC0001        0        Your Name
   _    SAP0001        0        Monthly Sales Report
   _    SAP0003        0        Requester
   _    SAP0004        0        Number of Copies
   _    SAP0005        0        Printer Output Queue

                                                            Bottom
   Parameters or command
   ===>  _____
   F3=Exit   F5=Refresh   F6=Add   F12=Cancel   F24=More keys
```

Figure 7.7 German Message File

```
                        Work with Message Descriptions
                                                       System: S1029115
    Message file:    SAMSG          Library:    GERLIB

    Position to . . . . . . .  _____     Message ID

    Type options, press Enter.
     2=Change    4=Delete    5=Display details    6=Print

    Opt  Message ID  Severity  Message Text
     _   SAC0001        0      Ihr Name
     _   SAP0001        0      Monatliche Umsatzstatistik
     _   SAP0003        0      Auftraggeber
     _   SAP0004        0      Anzahl der Kopien
     _   SAP0005        0      Drucker




                                                                  Bottom
    Parrameters or command
    ===>
    F3=Exit   F5=Refresh   F6=Add   F12=Cancel   F24=More keys
```

Figure 7.8 French Message File

```
                        Work with Message Descriptions
                                                       System: S1029115
    Message file:    SAMSG          Library:    FRNLIB

    Position to . . . . . . .  _____     Message ID

    Type options, press Enter.
     2=Change    4=Delete    5=Display details    6=Print

    Opt  Message ID  Severity  Message Text
     _   SAC0001        0      Votre Nom
     _   SAP0001        0      Logiciel de Ventes pour le Moi
     _   SAP0003        0      Requesteur
     _   SAP0004        0      Nombre de Copies
     _   SAP0005        0      Imprimente




                                                                  Bottom
    Parameters or command
    ===>
    F3=Exit   F5=Refresh   F6=Add   F12=Cancel   F24=More keys
```

When the user executes the command, the text is retrieved from the message file library in the user's library list. English-speaking users will see the screen shown in Figure 7.9, French-speaking users will see the prompt screen shown in Figure 7.10, and German-speaking users will see the screen shown in Figure 7.11.

Figure 7.9 Prompt Screen for English-Speaking Users

```
                      Monthly Sales Report (MONSARPT)

 Type choices, press Enter.

 Requester . . . . . . . . . .                  _____    Your Name
 Printer Output Queue. . . . .   QPRINT____
 Number of Copies. . . . . . .   1_             01-99




                                                                    Bottom
 F3=Exit   F4=Prompt   F5=Refresh   F12=Cancel   F13=How to use this display
 F24=More keys
```

Figure 7.10 Prompt Screen for French-Speaking Users

```
                    Logiciel de Ventes pour le Moi (MONSARPT)

 Type choices, press Enter.

 Requesteur . . . . . . . . . .                 _____    Votre Nom
 Imprimente . . . . . . . . . .   QPRINT____
 Nombre de Copies . . . . . . .   1_            01-99




                                                                    Bottom
 F3=Exit    F4=Prompt   F5=Refresh   F12=Cancel   F13=How to use this display
 F24=More keys
```

When you use message files, one set of application commands can support multiple language environments.

Figure 7.11 Prompt Screen for German-Speaking Users

```
                    Monatliche Umsatzstatistik (MONSARPT)

Type choices, press Enter.

Auftraggeber . . . . . . . . . .  _____        Ihr Name
Drucker. . . . . . . . . . . . :  QPRINT____
Anzahl der Kopien. . . . . . . .  1_             01-99












                                                               Bottom
F3=Exit   F4=Prompt   F5=Refresh   F12=Cancel   F13=How to use this display
F24=More keys
```

Message Files with DEP

Message files let you customize the error message for DEP dependent relationship errors.

You can also use message files with the DEP statement to determine the appropriate error message text. The DEP statement edits for a specified dependent relationship. The default message displayed when a dependency is not met is vague: "Requirements between parameters not satisfied," as shown in Figure 7.12.

Figure 7.12 Standard DEP Error Message

```
                        Copy Distribution Tape (TAATAPC)

Type choices, press Enter.

From device . . . . . . . . . .   TAP01_____   Name
To device . . . . . . . . . . .   TAP01_____   Name
To sequence number . . . . . . .  1             Number, *END
TODEV end of tape file option. .  *REWIND____   *LEAVE, *REWIND, *UNLOAD
Licensed programs to copy. . . .  *PROMPT____   *PROMPT, *ALL, 5738AAA-5728999
              + for more values   _____




                                                                     Bottom
F3=Exit   F4=Prompt   F5=Refresh   F12=Cancel   F13=How to use this display
F24=More keys
Requirements between parameters not satisfied.
```

Using a message file lets you tailor the message to the dependent relationship, thus making the message more descriptive. The following code is the command source code using a message identifier for the DEP error message, MSGID(USR0058):

```
CMD        PROMPT('Copy Distribution Tape')
PARM       KWD(FROMDEV) TYPE(*NAME) LEN(10) +
             MIN(1) EXPR(*YES) PROMPT('From device')
PARM       KWD(TODEV) TYPE(*NAME) LEN(10) +
             MIN(1) EXPR(*YES) PROMPT('To device')
PARM       KWD(TOSEQNBR) TYPE(*DEC) LEN(4 0) DFT(1) +
             SPCVAL((*END 0)) +
             PROMPT('To sequence number')
PARM       KWD(ENDOPT) TYPE(*CHAR) LEN(7) DFT(*REWIND) +
             RSTD(*YES) VALUES('*LEAVE' '*REWIND' +
             '*UNLOAD') +
             PROMPT('TODEV end of tape file option')
PARM       KWD(LICPGM) TYPE(*CHAR) LEN(7) +
             DFT(*PROMPT) RANGE('5738AAA' '5799999') +
             SNGVAL((*ALL)(*PROMPT)) MIN(0) MAX(200) +
             ALWUNPRT(*NO) FULL(*YES) EXPR(*YES) +
             CHOICE('*PROMPT, *ALL, 5738AAA-5728999') +
             PROMPT('Licensed programs to copy')
DEP        CTL(*ALWAYS) PARM((&FROMDEV *EQ &TODEV)) +
             NBRTRUE(*EQ 0) MSGID(USR0058)
```

The system will display the contents of a specified message when the dependent relationship described in the DEP statement is not true. In our example, the system will display USR0058 when input variables &FROMDEV and &TODEV are equal. Figure 7.13 shows how to add the custom text for the message, "From Device and To Device cannot be the same," to the message file.

Figure 7.13 Message File Identifier for DEP Error Text

```
                  Add Message Description (ADDMSGD)

Type choices, press Enter.

Message identifier . . . . . . .   USR0058___    Name
Message file . . . . . . . . . .   USRMSGF___    Name
  Library. . . . . . . . . . . .   *LIBL____     Name, *LIBL, *CURLIB
First-level message text . . . .   From Device and To Device cannot be the same

Second-level message text. . . .   *NONE_____
_____
_____
_____
_____
                                                                            ...

Severity code. . . . . . . . . .   00            0-99

                                                                       More...
F3=Exit   F4=Prompt   F5=Refresh   F10=Additional parameters   F12=Cancel
F13=How to use this display        F24=More keys
```

After you have created the message file with the necessary error messages, you can use those messages in your command. To create the link between the message file and your command, compile the command with the custom message file specified on the Message file parameter of the CRTCMD command (Figure 7.14).

When the user executes the command and the dependency error occurs, the system will retrieve the specified message from the message file and present it, as shown in Figure 7.15.

Figure 7.14 Specifying a Message File on the CRTCMD Command

```
                          Create Command (CRTCMD)

 Type choices, press Enter.

 Where allowed to run . . . . . .   *ALL           *ALL, *BATCH, *INTERACT...
                 + for more values
 Allow limited users. . . . . . .   *NO            *NO, *YES
 Maximum positional parameters. .   *NOMAX         0-75, *NOMAX
 Message file for prompt text . .   *NONE          Name, *NONE
   Library. . . . . . . . . . . .                  Name, *LIBL, *CURLIB
 Message file . . . . . . . . . .   USRMSGF        Name
   Library. . . . . . . . . . . .   *LIBL          Name, *LIBL, *CURLIB
 Help panel group . . . . . . . .   *NONE          Name, *NONE
   Library. . . . . . . . . . . .                  Name, *LIBL, *CURLIB
 Help identifier. . . . . . . . .   *NONE          Character value, *CMD, *NONE
 Help search index. . . . . . . .   *NONE          Name, *NONE, *SYSTEM
   Library. . . . . . . . . . . .                  Name, *LIBL, *CURLIB
 Current library. . . . . . . . .   *NOCHG         Name, *NOCHG, *CRTDFT
 Product library. . . . . . . . .   *NOCHG         Name, *NOCHG, *NONE

                                                                       More...
 F3=Exit   F4=Prompt   F5=Refresh   F12=Cancel   F13=How to read this display
```

Figure 7.15 Prompt Screen Displaying DEP Error Message

```
                       Copy Distribution Tape (TAATAPC)

 Type choices, press Enter.

  From device . . . . . . . . . .   TAP01          Name
  To device . . . . . . . . . . .   TAP01          Name
  To sequence number . . . . . . .  1              Number, *END
  TODEV end of tape file option. .  *REWIND        *LEAVE, *REWIND, *UNLOAD
  Licensed programs to copy. . . .  *PROMPT        *PROMPT, *ALL, 5738AAA-5728999
                 + for more values

                                                                       Bottom
 F3=Exit   F4=Prompt   F5=Refresh   F12=Cancel   F13=How to use this display
 F24=More keys
 From Device and To Device cannot be the same
```

Summary of Steps for Using Message Files

1. Create a message file (if one does not already exist).
2. Add messages to the message file.
3. Specify the message identifiers for the appropriate parameters.
4. Compile the command with the message files specified for the **Message file** and **Message file for prompt text** parameters.

Other PARM Statement Keywords

Chapter 8

We have seen many functions that the ubiquitous PARM command definition statement provides. Still other functions, although not as frequently used, provide even more flexibility and power to your programming toolkit. This chapter covers some of these additional powerful PARM keywords.

Special Values

The SPCVAL keyword lets you enter one parameter value, possibly a non-conforming value, but pass another value to the CPP.

You can use the special values (SPCVAL) keyword of the PARM statement to let users enter one value but pass a different value to the CPP. You can also use these special values to let users enter values that do not conform to the parameter type, such as *ALL for a *NAME type parameter (where * is usually not a valid first character).

You can enter up to 300 possible values for a PARM's SPCVAL keyword. This is not the same technique we use in the VALUES keyword, which also allows up to 300 possible values. The main difference between SPCVAL and VALUES is that the values on the VALUES keyword must conform to the attributes of the PARM; those of the SPCVAL keyword do not. The values specified for SPCVAL can be first converted to a value that does conform to the attributes of the PARM.

Application Example

Why would you want to use this technique? Suppose you are prompting a user for the information required to run a general ledger report. You are requesting an account number range (a **From account number** and a **Through account number**). You may want to give the user the option of entering an account number or a special value such as *START (to start at the beginning) or *END (to process through the last account number). Now *START and *END are not valid values for a numeric account number parameter. However, using SPCVAL, as shown in the code sample that follows, you can code the command so that the value of

*START will be passed to the CPP as 000000 and the value of *END will be passed to the CPP as 999999.

```
CMD         PROMPT('General Ledger Report')
PARM        KWD(WKMMYY) TYPE(*CHAR) LEN(4) RANGE(0100 +
              1299) MIN(1) FULL(*YES) CHOICE(MMYY) +
              PROMPT('Fiscal Period' 1)
PARM        KWD(WKREQ) TYPE(*CHAR) LEN(10) MIN(1) +
              CHOICE(*NONE) PROMPT(REQUESTER)
PARM        KWD(FRACCT) TYPE(*DEC) LEN(6) SPCVAL((*START +
              000000)) CHOICE(*VALUES) +
              PROMPT('From Account Number' 2)
PARM        KWD(TOACCT) TYPE(*DEC) LEN(6) SPCVAL((*END +
              999999)) CHOICE(*VALUES) +
              PROMPT('Through Account Number' 3)
PARM        KWD(WKOUTQ) TYPE(*CHAR) LEN(10) DFT(QPRINT) +
              CHOICE(*NONE) PROMPT('Printer Output Queue')
PARM        KWD(WKCOPY) TYPE(*CHAR) LEN(2) DFT(1) MIN(0) +
              CHOICE(*NONE) PROMPT('Number of Copies')
```

Coding SPCVAL

Look at the PARM statements for keywords FRACCT and TOACCT in the code above. Each of the SPCVAL keywords has two values, a **From** value and a **To** value. The **From** value represents what a user can enter. The **To** value is the value that the command passes to the CPP for that **From** value. If only a **From** value is entered, it is passed directly. So when the user enters *START for FRACCT, the command converts that value to 000000 and passes it to the CPP. The CPP never knows that anything but a normal account number was entered. You don't have to do any special coding in the CPP. The program fragment that follows shows these parameters coming in to the program from the command.

```
PGM                 PARM(&WKMMYY &RQSTR &FRACCT &TOACCT &OUTQ +
                      &COPIES)
/* DECLARE VARIABLES */
DCL                 VAR(&WKMMYY) TYPE(*CHAR) LEN(4)
DCL                 VAR(&RQSTR) TYPE(*CHAR) LEN(10)
DCL                 VAR(&FRACCT) TYPE(*CHAR) LEN(6)
DCL                 VAR(&TOACCT) TYPE(*CHAR) LEN(6)
DCL                 VAR(&OUTQ) TYPE(*CHAR) LEN(10)
DCL                 VAR(&COPIES) TYPE(*CHAR) LEN(2)
  .
  .
  .
```

The prompt screen this command generates is in Figure 8.1. Notice that the choice text (to the right of the input field) displays the values *START and *END as possible choices. This happens because we have specified the CHOICE(*VALUES) keyword, which is the default.

Figure 8.1 Prompt Screen Using Special Values

```
                    General Ledger Report (GLRPTCMD)

Type choices, press Enter.

Fiscal Period . . . . . . . . .    _____       MMYY
From Account Number . . . . . .    _____   Number, *START
Through Account Number. . . . .    _____   Number, *END
Requester . . . . . . . . . . .    _____
Printer Output Queue. . . . . .    QPRINT_____
Number of Copies. . . . . . . .    1_




                                                             Bottom
F3=Exit   F4=Prompt   F5=Refresh  F12=Cancel   F13=How to use this display
F24=More keys
```

SPCVAL with Mixed Lists

What if you specify **From** and **To** account numbers as a mixed list so that you can indent them nicely under a heading? The code is basically the same, but the SPCVAL keyword now appears in the ELEM statement that the PARM statement references.

```
.CMD        PROMPT('General Ledger Report')
            PARM        KWD(WKMMYY) TYPE(*CHAR) LEN(4) RANGE(0100 +
                          1299) MIN(1) FULL(*YES) CHOICE(MMYY) +
                          PROMPT('Fiscal Period')
            PARM        KWD(WKREQ) TYPE(*CHAR) LEN(10) MIN(1) +
                          CHOICE(*NONE) PROMPT(Requester)
            PARM        KWD(GLLIST) TYPE(GLELEM) +
                          PROMPT('Enter Range of Account Numbers:' 2)
            PARM        KWD(WKOUTQ) TYPE(*CHAR) LEN(10) DFT(QPRINT) +
                          CHOICE(*NONE) PROMPT('Printer Output Queue')
            PARM        KWD(WKCOPY) TYPE(*CHAR) LEN(2) DFT(1) MIN(0) +
                          CHOICE(*NONE) PROMPT('Number of Copies')
GLELEM:     ELEM        TYPE(*DEC) LEN(6) SPCVAL((*START +
                          000000)) PROMPT('From Account Number')
            ELEM        TYPE(*DEC) LEN(6) SPCVAL((*END +
                          999999)) PROMPT('Through Account Number')
```

Figure 8.2 shows the prompt screen with our range of account numbers specified as a mixed list.

Figure 8.2 Prompt Screen Using Special Values with a Mixed List

```
                    General Ledger Report (GLRPTCMD)

Type choices, press Enter.

Fiscal Period . . . . . . . . . . ____          MMYY
Enter Range of Acct Numbers:
From Account Number . . . . . . . _____        Number, *START
Through Account Number. . . . . . _____        Number, *END
Requester . . . . . . . . . . . . _____
Printer Output Queue. . . . . . . QPRINT____
Number of Copies. . . . . . . . . 1_


                                                              Bottom
F3=Exit    F4=Prompt    F5=Refresh    F12=Cancel    F13=How to use this display
F24=More keys
```

Another Example

Use SPCVAL to allow the user to enter abbreviated parameter values.

A common reason to use SPCVAL is to let the user enter an abbreviated version of a value. For example, when prompting for a source file name, instead of forcing users to key the entire name for a standard IBM source file name (such as QCLSRC), you can let them key a short code (such as CL). The following code shows an example of this use of SPCVAL:

```
           CMD       PROMPT('Find SBMJOB')
           PARM      KWD(MBR) TYPE(QUAL1) PROMPT('Source Member +
                       Name')
           PARM      KWD(UPDREF) TYPE(*CHAR) LEN(1) RSTD(*YES) +
                       DFT(N) VALUES(Y N) PROMPT('Update PGMREF +
                       File?')
           PARM      KWD(REFILE) TYPE(QUAL2) PMTCTL(CONDITION1) +
                       PROMPT('PGMREF File Name')
QUAL1:     QUAL      TYPE(*NAME) LEN(10) DFT(*ALL) SPCVAL((*ALL))
           QUAL      TYPE(*NAME) LEN(10) DFT(CL) SPCVAL((RPG +
                       QRPGSRC) (CL QCLSRC) (DDS QDDSSRC)) +
                       PROMPT('Source File Name')
           QUAL      TYPE(*NAME) LEN(10) PROMPT('Library Name')
QUAL2:     QUAL      TYPE(*NAME) LEN(10)
           QUAL      TYPE(*NAME) LEN(10) PROMPT('PGMREF Library +
                       Name')
CONDITION1: PMTCTL   CTL(UPDREF) COND((*EQ Y))
```

In the example, the qualifying parameter for the source file name specifies three sets of SPCVAL — RPG, CL, and DDS. The user may enter RPG, CL, DDS, or any source file name. If the user enters one of the special values, such as RPG, the command will translate it to the corresponding file name (in this case, QRPGSRC) and pass that name to the CPP.

Because we have not specified the CHOICE keyword, the default value of *VALUES will be used, and the special values will appear as the CHOICE text (Figure 8.3).

Figure 8.3 Using SPCVAL to Abbreviate Values

```
                         Find SBMJOB (FNDSBM)

Type choices, press Enter.

Source Member Name. . . . . .     *ALL         Name, *ALL
    Source File Name. . . . . .     CL           Name, RPG, CL, DDS
Library Name. . . . . . . . .                  Name
Update PGMREF File? . . . . .     N            Y, N











                                                          Bottom
F3=Exit  F4=Prompt   F5=Refresh   F12=Cancel   F13=How to use this display
F24=More keys
```

When a user presses F4 to prompt for a list of values, the values specified on the SPCVAL keyword will appear as shown in Figure 8.4.

*SPCVAL passes to the CPP the name of the current library when you specify *CURLIB as the to value.*

Here is a final tidbit about using SPCVAL. If *CURLIB is specified as the **To** value for SPCVAL, the name of the current job library is passed to the CPP. For example, if you specify a special value of SPCVAL(CUR *CURLIB) to let the user enter a shorthand version of *CURLIB, the command will not pass the *CURLIB to the CPP; rather, it will pass the library name that is the current library when the user executes the command.

Figure 8.4 List of Values Displayed by F4

```
                         Specify Value for Parameter MBR

  Type CHOICE, press Enter.

  Type . . . . . . . . . . . . . . :      NAME
  CL File Name . . . . . . . . . .        QCLSRC_____

    RPG
    CL
    DDS








  F3=Exit   F5=Refresh   F12=Cancel   F13=How to use this display   F24=More keys
```

Many Commands, One CPP...

Using the CONST keyword, you can write one CPP or one validity checking program to serve many commands.

Every command requires a CPP to perform the actual function fronted by the command prompt screen. Generally, you write a CPP for each command. The special technique we cover in this section will show you how to write one CPP that you can then use to process multiple commands. This technique uses the PARM statement's CONSTANT keyword. The CONSTANT keyword of the PARM command-definition statement lets you pass a specific fixed value (a constant) for the PARM. This PARM is not displayed on the prompt screen but is internal to the command (therefore, you cannot specify prompt text for it).

You can use the CONSTANT keyword to let one CPP or validity-checking program process several different commands. The validity checker, which we cover in Chapter 12, is simply a program that the command calls to perform additional editing on the parameters. Both the CPP and the validity checker receive the parameters from the command. Typically one CPP and one validity-checking program serve a single command. However, if several commands share many common parameters (which happens often within a single application), it is often more efficient to write a single CPP or a single validity-checking program to accommodate the similar commands than to write a separate program for each command.

To create a placeholder parameter, use CONSTANT(' ').

If you use the CONSTANT keyword with a value of **blank**, you can use a single CPP or validity-checking program with multiple commands. CONSTANT(' ') makes a PARM a dummy parameter that acts merely as a place holder in a list of PARMs. If you write the validity-checking program to process 10 possible parameters, but a particular command uses only seven of those parameters, you use CONSTANT(' ') to define those three dummy parameters. The three place-holder parameters ensure that the command passes the correct number of parameters in the proper sequence.

Example of Validity-Checking Program

Let's look at an example. Suppose your sales analysis application provides three reports. These reports prompt the user for various parameters, many of which are used on all three reports. When you review the three reports, you identify seven parameters that need to be edited in a validity-checking program. These seven parameters are shown below, in the order in which the validity-checking program processes them.

- Division
- Warehouse
- Market
- Territory
- Salesperson
- Customer
- OUTQ

In your application, you find three programs that prompt for various combinations of these parameters. As shown in Figure 8.5, Program A uses Division, Warehouse and OUTQ; Program B uses Market, Territory, Salesperson, Customer and OUTQ; and Program C uses all seven parameters.

Figure 8.5 Programs Using the Parameters

Parameters by Program		
Program A	**Program B**	**Program C**
Division	Market	Division
Warehouse	Territory	Warehouse
OUTQ	Salesperson	Market
	Customer	Territory
	OUTQ	Salesperson
		Customer
		OUTQ

For three of these commands to use the same validity-checking program, dummy place-holder parameters must be passed to the validity checker for the missing parameters, as shown in Figure 8.6.

Figure 8.6 Command Parameters and Placeholders

Parameters by Program with Placeholders		
Program A	**Program B**	**Program C**
Division	*N	Division
Warehouse	*N	Warehouse
*N	Market	Market
*N	Territory	Territory
*N	Salesperson	Salesperson
*N	Customer	Customer
OUTQ	OUTQ	OUTQ

You define the commands for these three reports with CONSTANT (' ') for the dummy parameters. Following is the command source code for command A.

```
CMD         PROMPT('Monthly Sales Reports A')
PARM        KWD(WKDIV) TYPE(*CHAR) LEN(2) +
              CHOICE('(Blank for ALL Div)') +
              PROMPT('Division')
PARM        KWD(WKWH) TYPE(*CHAR) LEN(3) +
              CHOICE('(Blank for ALL Warehouses)') +
              PROMPT('Warehouse')
PARM        KWD(WKMKT) TYPE(*CHAR) LEN(1) CONSTANT(' ')
PARM        KWD(WKTERR) TYPE(*CHAR) LEN(2) CONSTANT(' ')
PARM        KWD(WKSM) TYPE(*CHAR) LEN(5) CONSTANT(' ')
PARM        KWD(WKCUST) TYPE(*CHAR) LEN(6) +
              CONSTANT(' ')
PARM        KWD(WKOUTQ) TYPE(*CHAR) LEN(10) DFT(QPRINT) +
              CHOICE(*NONE) PROMPT('Printer OUTQ')
```

The four dummy parameters (WKMKT, WKTERR, WKSM, and WKCUST) all have CONSTANT(' ') specified. The resulting prompt screen is shown in Figure 8.7.

Figure 8.7 Prompt Screen for Command A

```
                        Monthly Sales Reports A (SARPTACMD)

 Type choices, press Enter.

 Division. . . . . . . . . . . .     __          (Blank for ALL Div)
 Warehouse . . . . . . . . . . .     __          (Blank for ALL Warehouses)
 Printer OUTQ. . . . . . . . .      QPRINT____







                                                                    Bottom
 F3=Exit   F4=Prompt   F5=Refresh   F12=Cancel   F13=How to use this display
 F24=More keys
```

Although the dummy parameters do not appear on the screen, they are passed to the validity-checking program (as blanks), thus enabling one program to accommodate several different commands.

Example with CPP

Using CONST, you can pass the name of the command to the CPP.

You can use this same method to allow a single CPP to process multiple commands. In this case, you pass a constant parameter containing the name of the command so your CPP will know which command it is processing, in order to perform the appropriate function. In the following code sample, we have added another CONSTANT parameter to pass that information to the CPP.

```
CMD       PROMPT('Monthly Sales Reports A')
PARM      KWD(WKDIV) TYPE(*CHAR) LEN(2) MIN(0) +
            CHOICE('(Blank for ALL Div)') +
            PROMPT('Division')
PARM      KWD(WKWH) TYPE(*CHAR) LEN(3) MIN(0) +
            CHOICE('(Blank for ALL Warehouses)') +
            PROMPT('Warehouse')
PARM      KWD(WKMKT) TYPE(*CHAR) LEN(1) CONSTANT(' ')
PARM      KWD(WKTERR) TYPE(*CHAR) LEN(2) CONSTANT(' ')
PARM      KWD(WKSM) TYPE(*CHAR) LEN(5) CONSTANT(' ')
PARM      KWD(WKCUST) TYPE(*CHAR) LEN(6) +
            CONSTANT(' ')
PARM      KWD(WKOUTQ) TYPE(*CHAR) LEN(10) DFT(QPRINT) +
            CHOICE(*NONE) PROMPT('Printer OUTQ')
PARM      KWD(CMDCD) TYPE(*CHAR) LEN(4) CONSTANT('CMDA')
```

Each command passes a different constant in the eighth parameter so that the CPP will know which specific actions to take.

Creating Commands Without a CPP

You can use CONST to create commands that use IBM's QCMDEXC as the CPP.

You can also use the CONSTANT keyword to create commands that will execute IBM's QCMDEXC API, therefore relieving you of the task of writing a CPP. QCMDEXC is an IBM program that lets you execute commands. QCMDEXC is frequently used in HLL programs to process a CL command; for example, you can perform an OVRPRTF (Override with Printer File) command from within an RPG program.

Example with QCMDEXC

To use this technique, you use the CONSTANT parameter to define a PARM that contains the function to perform. For example, to work with all jobs submitted from the workstation, you create the constant, WRKSBMJOB *WRKSTN, and pass it to QCMDEXC. QCMDEXC will in turn execute the WRKSBMJOB command with the *WRKSTN parameter. Programmers and operators use this type of function to create short-cut macros that make their life easier (and take the strain off their keying fingers). If you are an operator who keys WRKSBMJOB *WRKSTN 20 or 30 times a day, reducing the command to WS is a significant time saver. Let's look at this technique and how easily you can create such macros.

To use QCMDEXC, you must pass it two parameters. The first parameter contains the command to execute, including all that command's parameters. The second parameter contains the length of the character string of the first parameter. The first parameter must be TYPE(*CHAR). The second parameter must be TYPE(*DEC), LEN(15 5).

The following source code shows the command source statements to create our example macro — a short-form command to work with jobs submitted from the workstation.

```
CMD      PROMPT('WRKSBMJOB From Workstation')
PARM     KWD(CMD) TYPE(*CHAR) LEN(17) +
           CONSTANT('WRKSBMJOB *WRKSTN')
PARM     KWD(LENGTH) TYPE(*DEC) LEN(15 5) CONSTANT(17)
```

The first PARM (CMD) contains the fixed value WRKSMBJOB *WRKSTN. The second PARM (LENGTH) contains the value of the number of characters in the first PARM (17). These parameters will be passed to QCMDEXC. Then, when compiling this command with CRTCMD, you specify QCMDEXC as the CPP, as shown in Figure 8.8.

Figure 8.8 Using QCMDEXC as the CPP

```
                          Create Command (CRTCMD)

Type choices, press Enter.

Command . . . . . . . . . . . .   WS_____    Name
  Library . . . . . . . . . .       *CURLIB___  Name, *CURLIB
Program to process command. . .   QCMDEXC___    Name, *REXX
  Library . . . . . . . . . .       *LIBL_____  Name, *LIBL, *CURLIB
Source file . . . . . . . . . .   COMMANDS__    Name
  Library . . . . . . . . . .       LNLIB_____  Name, *LIBL, *CURLIB
Source member . . . . . . . . .   WS_____    Name, *CMD
Text 'description'. . . . . . .   *SRCMBRTXT_____



Additional Parameters

Replace command . . . . . . . .   *YES          *YES, *NO


                                                                Bottom
F3=Exit   F4=Prompt   F5=Refresh   F10=Additional parameters   F12=Cancel
F13=How to use this display        F24=More keys
```

The CONST value cannot exceed 32 characters in length.

When you execute this command (by simply keying WS), the two parameters are passed to QCMDEXC, which in turn executes the character string in the first PARM. You can use this technique to create an almost unlimited number of simple command macros without a special CPP. One limitation can be severe in certain situations: The value of the CONSTANT keyword cannot exceed 32 characters. That is not a lot of characters when you are defining commands, so keep this limitation in mind and remember that this technique will not work in every situation.

Example with System Command

As a final example, the following code demonstrates a handy CPP-less command to display the time:

```
CMD        PROMPT('Display Time')
PARM       KWD(CMD) TYPE(*CHAR) LEN(15) +
              CONSTANT('DSPSYSVAL QTIME')
PARM       KWD(LENGTH) TYPE(*DEC) LEN(15 5) CONSTANT(15)
```

Selective Prompting

Chapter 9

*Selective prompting
characters allow you to
customize the prompting of
certain command
parameters.*

Selective prompting is a technique that allows dynamic customization of existing commands without changing the source. The technique determines which parameters are prompted and what values they display. You can use selective prompting with interactive prompting for both IBM-supplied commands and custom-written commands. Selective prompting adds another layer of usefulness to commands. You are not limited to using existing commands without modification; you can easily tailor them to your needs.

Displaying Prompts from Menu Options

Let's begin with the basics. Sometimes you want to put a command you have written (or one of IBM's) behind a menu item. How do you display the command's prompt screen every time a user selects that menu item? You simply place a **?** in front of the command name in the menu file or CL program. For example, to display the command prompt screen for a command called PRTRPT, you create the menu option as ?PRTRPT. Using the **?** is the same as using F4 (prompt) from the command line, but with the **?**, users do not have the option of not seeing the prompt screen. Every time they take the F4 menu option, the system displays the command prompt screen.

However, life is not always that simple. Sometimes you want to let a user run a certain command without providing access to *all* the parameters for that command. A technique called selective prompting lets you limit access to only certain parameters by placing special characters, called selective prompt characters, in front of the individual parameter keywords.

Selective Prompt Characters

Let's look at an example using IBM's WRKUSRJOB command. This command will display the Work with User Jobs panel for a selected user.

If we use ?WRKUSRJOB behind a menu option, the entire WRKUSRJOB command is displayed, as shown in Figure 9.1.

Figure 9.1 Standard WRKUSRJOB Command

```
                    Work with User Jobs (WRKUSRJOB)

Type choices, press Enter.

User whose jobs to display . . .   *            Name, *, *ALL
Status of user jobs. . . . . . .   *ALL         *ALL, *ACTIVE, *JOBQ, *OUTQ
Output . . . . . . . . . . . . .   *            *, *PRINT
Job type . . . . . . . . . . . .   *ALL         *ALL, *INTERACT, *BATCH




                                                                   Bottom
F3=Exit   F4=Prompt   F5=Refresh   F10=Additional parameters   F12=Cancel
F13=How to use this display        F24=More keys
```

However, we want the users to work only with their own jobs, so we do not want to let them change the **User whose jobs to display** prompt. We also want them to see only batch jobs, so we want to force a specific value to the **Job type** prompt and not let the users change it. And we do not want them to be able to select *PRINT as the output — we only want them to be able to display the jobs on their screen. Essentially, the only option in the WRKUSRJOB command that we want users to access is the **Status of user jobs** parameter. To accomplish this limitation, we use the selective prompting form of the WRKUSRJOB command that follows:

```
WRKUSRJOB     ??STATUS() JOBTYPE(*BATCH)
```

The two special characters (**??**) in front of the STATUS keyword are examples of selective prompt characters. They tell the system how to handle the parameter. For example,

- to select a parameter for display: ??KEYWORD()
- to omit a parameter from display: ?-KEYWORD()
- to display and protect a parameter: ?*KEYWORD()

In the example WRKUSRJOB command above, the system will display the STATUS parameter and let the user enter a value. If we want to display the parameter without letting the user change the value, we use ?*STATUS().

How we specify the parameter value also has an effect on how the system will handle the prompting. A parameter value can follow the parameter keyword in parentheses. A value of () will cause the command's default value to be used. A value of (*XXX*) will cause the value *XXX* to be used. In our example, the system will display STATUS with its default value (*ALL). Figure 9.2 shows the selectively prompted command.

Figure 9.2 Selectively Prompted WRKUSRJOB

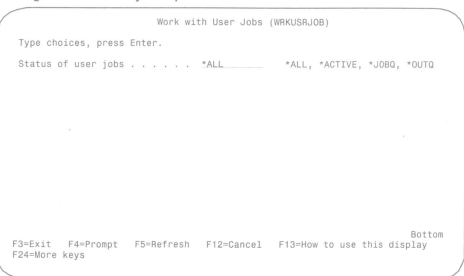

```
                         Work with User Jobs (WRKUSRJOB)

 Type choices, press Enter.

 Status of user jobs . . . . . .   *ALL_____     *ALL, *ACTIVE, *JOBQ, *OUTQ












                                                                       Bottom
 F3=Exit    F4=Prompt   F5=Refresh   F12=Cancel   F13=How to use this display
 F24=More keys
```

Notice that the JOBTYPE parameter is not displayed. The command will use the value that we give it in the command (*BATCH). All other parameters in the command will not be displayed but will be processed with their defaults.

Selective Prompting Options

As you can see, we have several options for controlling the prompting of a command. The first is to force the system to prompt all the command parameters all the time. For this option, use the ? in front of the command. If, however, you want to selectively prompt parts of the command, use the individual selective prompt characters for each parameter you want to prompt. If at least one parameter is specified for selective prompt, only the specified parameters are displayed. It's like telling the system you want control — once you specify one parameter, you have control over the prompting variations of all the parameters.

The chart in Table 9.1 (from IBM's *CL Programmers Guide*) summarizes the selective prompt characters.

Table 9.1 Selective Prompt Chart

Selective Prompt Characters	
Characters	**Description**
??	The parameter is displayed and input capable.
?*	The parameter is displayed but is not input capable. Any user-specified value will be passed to the command processing program.
?<	The parameter is displayed and is input capable, but the command default is sent to the CPP unless the value displayed on the parameter is changed.
?/	Reserved for IBM use.
?-	The parameter is not displayed. The specified value (or default) is passed to the CPP. Not allowed in prompt-override programs.
?&	The parameter is not displayed until F9=All parameters is pressed. Once displayed, it is input capable. The command default is sent to the CPP unless the value displayed on the parameter is changed.
?%	The parameter is not displayed until F9=All parameters is pressed. Once displayed, it is not input-capable. The command default is sent to the CPP.

Selective Prompting with SBMJOB

Let's look at some more examples to get a feeling for the variety available with this technique. Suppose you want to let the user submit a job to run a query. You begin with IBM's SBMJOB command and then add selective prompting. The SBMJOB command has myriad parameters, of which you want to use only three. The user needs only to specify the query to run, the job name to use (to uniquely identify the request), and the output queue to which to print. You use the selective prompt that follows:

```
SBMJOB        ??CMD(RUNQRY LIBRARY/QUERY) ??JOB() ??OUTQ()
```

This command results in the prompt screen shown in Figure 9.3.

The command to run (RUNQRY LIBRARY/QUERY) appears with the specified values. This command merely acts as a mask or template for the user; the default values of LIBRARY and QUERY are not really object names, but they assist the user in entering the actual values for the query and library. The **Job name** parameter is displayed with the command's default value, as is the OUTQ parameter. The system displays no other SBMJOB parameters because they were not specified. All the other parameters will use their default values.

Figure 9.3 Selective Prompt Screen to Submit a RUNQRY Command

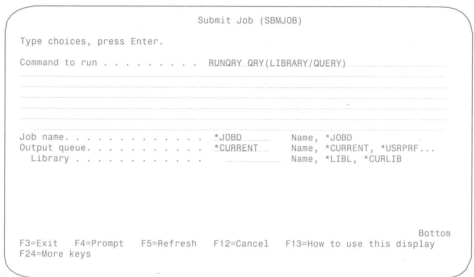

```
                                Submit Job (SBMJOB)

 Type choices, press Enter.

 Command to run . . . . . . . .   RUNQRY QRY(LIBRARY/QUERY)


 Job name. . . . . . . . . . . .   *JOBD         Name, *JOBD
 Output queue. . . . . . . . . .   *CURRENT      Name, *CURRENT, *USRPRF...
   Library . . . . . . . . . . .                 Name, *LIBL, *CURLIB




                                                                       Bottom
 F3=Exit   F4=Prompt   F5=Refresh   F12=Cancel   F13=How to use this display
 F24=More keys
```

If you want to change the default of one parameter but do not want to display the parameter to the user, you can specify the parameter with the desired value, as we did with JOBTYPE in the example WRKUSRJOB command on page 90. The system will take the value and, as long as you have specified at least one selective prompt character, will use that value without prompting the parameter.

Dynamic Defaults

You can also use selective prompting to dynamically default values on the prompt screen. For example, when presenting a command prompt screen to run a report, you can load the **Requester** parameter with the user ID as a default (what is displayed), as shown in the following code, where a variable is used instead of a constant:

```
PRTPRT      RQSTR(&USERID)
```

Selective Prompting with QCMDEXC

Our final example in this chapter is one that combines the selective prompting technique with the technique we discussed in Chapter 8 — using QCMDEXC as the CPP. Suppose that you have a query that reports the daily sales in a summary form for your sales manager. The report is designed to run at the end of the day so the manager can have a snapshot of the day's sales activities. Now, however, the manager wants to be able to check sales anytime during the day and display the report rather than print it.

Your solution is a simple one. Use a command that submits the RUNQRY command to QCMDEXC and prompts for the FORMTYPE so the manager can select either *DISPLAY or *PRINT. The following command will do the trick:

```
CMD         PROMPT('Daily Sales Summary')
PARM        KWD(CMD) TYPE(*CHAR) LEN(31) +
            CONSTANT ('RUNQRY QRY(QSLSNOW) ??OUTTYPE()')
PARM        KWD(LENGTH) TYPE(*DEC) LEN(15 5) CONSTANT(31
```

Remember, however, the limitation on the CONSTANT keyword. You cannot specify a value that is longer than 32 characters. If you get into any kind of elaborate command, this technique will not work.

Changing Commands and Command Defaults

Chapter 10

In some situations, you will need to make minor changes to existing commands. Two commands, CHGCMD (Change Command) and CHGCMDDFT (Change Command Default), enable these kinds of changes.

Changing Command Attributes

The CHGCMD command lets you change many attributes of a command, including the name of the CPP.

You specify a command's attributes (such as the CPP) when you execute CRTCMD to compile the command source member into the command definition object. You can alter many of these attributes without recompiling the command by using the CHGCMD command. Some attributes that you can change are

- the CPP
- the validity-checking program
- the type of job from which the command may be run
- the help panel group
- the prompt override program

The Advanced Topics section of this book discusses the purpose of these attributes.

CHGCMD with Custom Commands

Let's look at one example of when the CHGCMD command can be helpful. You might want to use the CHGCMD command after you compile a command and then discover that you forgot to change the CPP to your CPP program name. You can recompile the command; however, the CHGCMD command as shown in Figure 10.1 is much quicker.

Figure 10.1 Using the CHGCMD Command to Change the CPP

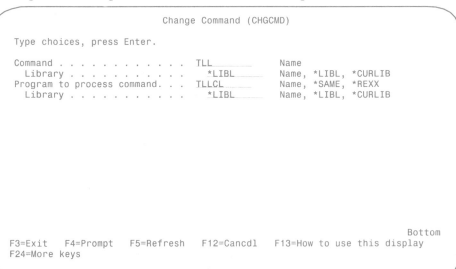

```
                          Change Command (CHGCMD)

 Type choices, press Enter.

 Command  . . . . . . . . . . . .   TLL           Name
   Library  . . . . . . . . . . .     *LIBL       Name, *LIBL, *CURLIB
 Program to process command. . .    TLLCL         Name, *SAME, *REXX
   Library  . . . . . . . . . .       *LIBL       Name, *LIBL, *CURLIB




                                                                   Bottom
 F3=Exit   F4=Prompt   F5=Refresh   F12=Cancel   F13=How to use this display
 F24=More keys
```

CHGCMD with IBM Commands

You may want to change an IBM-supplied command from time to time.
You can use CHGCMD with IBM-supplied commands, as well as with
custom-defined commands, although you must be careful. *Never change
IBM commands' CPPs, validity-checking programs, or prompt-override
programs if you want them to continue to work properly.*

*Use CHGCMD to force a
command to run in batch.*

    IBM's RUNQRY (Run Query) command is a prime candidate for
change. When run interactively, RUNQRY frequently causes havoc
because it can be such a resource hog. You can use CHGCMD to
prevent the command from running interactively. Figure 10.2 shows the
CHGCMD used on RUNQRY. The **Where allowed to run** parameter
indicates which types of jobs (e.g., batch, interactive) may run this
command. Simply eliminate the values for interactive (e.g.,
*INTERACT, *IPGM), and queries can no longer run interactively
(not even if you press F5 when working in a query).

Figure 10.2 Using the CHGCMD Command to Change RUNQRY

```
                          Change Command (CHGCMD)

 Type choices, press Enter.

 Command . . . . . . . . . . . .   RUNQRY_____     Name
   Library . . . . . . . . . . .   *LIBL_____    Name, *LIBL, *CURLIB
 Program to process command. . .   QQUDA_____    Name, *SAME, *REXX
   Library . . . . . . . . . . .   *LIBL_____    Name, *LIBL, *CURLIB
 Validity checking program . . .   *NONE_____    Name, *SAME, *NONE
   Library . . . . . . . . . . .   _____    Name, *LIBL, *CURLIB
 Mode in which valid . . . . . .   *PROD_____    *SAME, *ALL, *PROD, *DEBUG...
                                   *DEBUG____
                                   *SERVICE__
 Where allowed to run . . . . . .  *IREXX____    *SAME, ALL, *BATCH...
                                   *BREXX____
                                   *BPGM_____
                                   *IPGM_____
                                   *EXEC_____
                                   *INTERACT_
                                   *BATCH____
                                                                    More...
 F3=Exit    F4=Prompt    F5=Refresh    F12=Cancel    F13=How to use this display
 F24=More keys
```

Keep in mind that changes to IBM commands will remain in effect only until the next time the operating system is loaded. Reloading the operating system (such as during a release upgrade) will replace the changed versions of the commands with IBM's original versions. You must then use CHGCMD again to change them. Alternatively, you can keep copies of the changed IBM commands in a special library that resides at the top of all system library lists. This latter method, however, may cause a potential problem. If a new release of the operating system is installed and the IBM commands that you modified have been changed for that new release, your modified commands may not work due to parameter mismatches between your old modified command and the new CPP, prompt-override program, or validity-checking program.

Changing Command Defaults

The CHGCMDDFT command lets you change the default values for a command's parameters.

In addition to changing a command's attributes, you can change the default values for the parameters of a command without changing the command source. The CHGCMDDFT command provides this function. You can use this command for both IBM and custom commands. The main restriction is that the new default value must conform to the attributes of its parameter (e.g., type, length). Also, you can change only the default value of parameters that have default values (you cannot add a default value where one does not already exist).

Default values may be changed for parameters (PARM), elements in a list (ELEM), or qualified names (QUAL). The following examples illustrate how you might use the CHGCMDDFT command to change the default values of existing commands.

An Example with CRTCLPGM

IBM's CRTCLPGM (Create CL Program) command will compile a CL program using established defaults. If you find that you change the values of the defaults every time you create a CL program, you may want to change the CRTCLPGM defaults instead. Figure 10.3 shows an example of changing the **User Profile** and **Log Level** parameters of CRTCLPGM. Use the keyword(s) you want to change, followed by the new default value.

Figure 10.3 Changing Some Defaults of IBM's CRTCLPGM Command

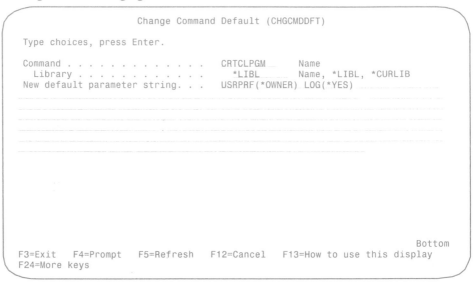

```
                          Change Command Default (CHGCMDDFT)

 Type choices, press Enter.

 Command . . . . . . . . . . . . .    CRTCLPGM__    Name
   Library . . . . . . . . . . . .      *LIBL____   Name, *LIBL, *CURLIB
 New default parameter string. . .    USRPRF(*OWNER) LOG(*YES) _____

 _____
 _____
 _____
 _____
 _____






                                                                   Bottom
 F3=Exit   F4=Prompt   F5=Refresh   F12=Cancel   F13=How to use this display
 F24=More keys
```

An Example with CRTPF

Another example is IBM's CRTPF (Create Physical File) command, which creates a physical file. The default value for **Maximum number of records** is 10,000. Most programmers prefer to create a file with *NOMAX for the number of records to avoid those unwelcome midnight phone calls. Figure 10.4 shows how to change the default value of the CRTPF command to *NOMAX.

Figure 10.4 Changing the Default Value of CRTPF Command

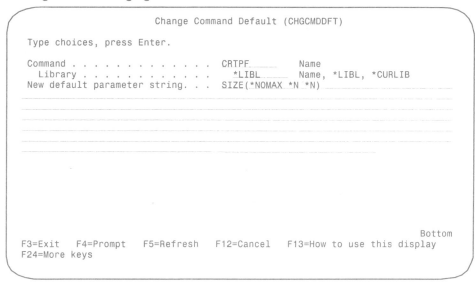

```
                      Change Command Default (CHGCMDDFT)

 Type choices, press Enter.

 Command . . . . . . . . . . . . .   CRTPF        Name
   Library . . . . . . . . . . .       *LIBL        Name, *LIBL, *CURLIB
 New default parameter string. . .   SIZE(*NOMAX *N *N)




                                                                    Bottom
 F3=Exit   F4=Prompt   F5=Refresh   F12=Cancel   F13=How to use this display
 F24=More keys
```

Because the **Maximum number of records** parameter is part of a mixed list, we use place holders (*N) to skip the elements of the list that we do not want to change.

The same caveats that applied to changing IBM commands with the CHGCMD command apply equally to CHGCMDDFT. That is, the changes will be overlaid when you reload the operating system. If you are creating your own copies of the commands in a special library, you may run into trouble when IBM changes its version so that the IBM version is no longer compatible with your older version.

Section 3

Advanced Topics

Choice Exit Programs

Chapter 11

On a CL command prompt screen, the choice text (the text displayed to the right of the parameter) and the permissible values list (displayed when F4 is pressed) can come from four possible sources, determined by the value of the CHOICE keyword of the PARM statement. First, the text can be hard-coded in the keyword, as in CHOICE('XXXXXXX'). This is the simplest way to specify the choice text.

Second, you can specify a message identifier, as in CHOICE(MSG0001). We discussed this in Chapter 7, "Message Files." You use this technique when messages might be used in multiple commands. You might also specify a message identifier when, as in our foreign language example, you want to dynamically select between different messages.

The third technique bases the choice text on the values specified in the PARM statement as the default, range, special value, and so on. With this method, by specifying CHOICE(*VALUES), you can cause each possible value to appear automatically. See Chapter 2, "Defining Parameters," for more information about this technique.

Choice exit programs let you dynamically retrieve values for a command parameter.

The fourth method for determining a parameter's choice text is to use a choice exit program. Such a program can dynamically retrieve values that the command in turn will display on the command prompt screen and on the permissible values list. This method is very useful when you are prompting for volatile values that are stored in a data file.

Two steps are involved when you use a choice exit program. You first must write the choice exit program (in any language). Then you define the program on the CHOICE keyword by specifying CHOICE(*PGM) on the PARM, ELEM, or QUAL statement and specifying the program name for the CHOICEPGM keyword.

Defining a Choice Exit Program in a Command

Let's look at an example. Figure 11.1 shows a command in which several of the PARMs use a choice exit program. You can write a single choice exit program for a specific parameter and then specify that program in all the commands in which that parameter is used. This makes your effort worthwhile and the choice exit program very efficient to use. Notice in the command below that each choice exit program is unique to the parameter for which it is specified. Unlike with the CPP, you specify the name of the choice exit program directly in the PARM statement, not in the CRTCMD command.

Figure 11.1 Command Using Choice Exit Programs

```
CMD         PROMPT('Comp Price Comparison Report')
PARM        KWD(COMP#) TYPE(*CHAR) LEN(6) MIN(0) +
              CHOICE(*PGM) CHOICEPGM(CHCCOMP) +
              PROMPT('Competitor #')
PARM        KWD(BRAND) TYPE(*CHAR) LEN(2) MIN(0) +
              CHOICE(*PGM) CHOICEPGM(CHCBRND) +
              PROMPT('Product Brand')
PARM        KWD(CLASS) TYPE(*CHAR) LEN(2) MIN(0) +
              CHOICE(*PGM) CHOICEPGM(CHCCLS) +
              PROMPT('Product Class')
PARM        KWD(ABCCD) TYPE(*CHAR) LEN(1) MIN(0) +
              CHOICE('(blank for ALL ABC Codes)') +
              PROMPT('ABC Code')
PARM        KWD(PRCCD) TYPE(*CHAR) LEN(1) RSTD(*YES) +
              DFT(J) VALUES('W' 'J' 'O') MIN(0) +
              CHOICE('(W=WD, J=Jobber, O=Other)') +
              PROMPT('Competitor''s Price')
PARM        KWD(PRCLST) TYPE(*CHAR) LEN(8) RSTD(*NO) +
              MIN(0) CHOICE(*NONE) PROMPT('Our Price List')
PARM        KWD(WH) TYPE(*CHAR) LEN(3) RSTD(*NO) DFT(80) +
              MIN(0) CHOICE(*PGM) CHOICEPGM(CHCWH) +
              PROMPT('WAREHOUSE (for ABC Code)')
PARM        KWD(OUTQ) TYPE(*CHAR) LEN(10) RSTD(*NO) +
              DFT(QPRINT) MIN(0) CHOICE(*PGM) +
              CHOICEPGM(CHCOUTQ) PROMPT('Printer OUTQ')
PARM        KWD(REQUESTER) TYPE(*CHAR) LEN(10) RSTD(*NO) +
              MIN(0) CHOICE(*NONE) PROMPT(REQUESTER)
PARM        KWD(COPIES) TYPE(*CHAR) LEN(2) DFT(01) +
              RANGE('01' '99') MIN(0) CHOICE('(01 - +
              99)') PROMPT('Number of Copies')
```

The Choice Exit Program

Remember that the choice exit program determines both the choice text (displayed to the right of the parameter) and the permissible values list (displayed when F4 is pressed). The program can be written in any high-level language, and the program must process two parameters. The first

---

parameter contains the data that is passed from the command to the choice exit program. The second parameter will hold the data that is passed from the choice exit program back to the command.

Choice Exit Program Parameters

Choice exit program parameters are transparent to the command. You do not define them anywhere in the command — you just have to know their layout and code the choice exit program accordingly. The first parameter, the one that is passed to the choice exit program, consists of three fields. The first field contains the command name. The second field contains the name of the keyword of the PARM being processed. The third field contains a one-character code that indicates whether the data to be returned to the command is for the choice text (C) or for the permissible values list (P). Figure 11.2. summarizes this parameter.

Figure 11.2 Structure of First Choice Exit Program Parameter

Position	
1 - 10	Command Name
11 - 20	Keyword Name
21 - 21	Return Code (C or P)

As soon as the user executes the command, the system passes the first parameter to the choice exit program with a C in the return code. The program must then build the choice text to be displayed on the prompt screen. If the user presses F4 with the cursor on the specified field, the system calls the choice exit program again, this time with a P in the return code. The choice exit program then builds the list of valid entries for the parameter and displays them on the F4 prompt screen. The user may key the desired value on this screen, press Enter, and return to the main prompt screen with the selected value loaded in the parameter. It is important to remember that the list of permissible values is simply a list of *possible* values, not a finite list of *valid* values. The user may enter a value that is not in the list. You must use other means to edit the entered values.

The second parameter, which holds the data returned to the command, is a 30-byte field containing the choice text if the return code is C, or a 2000-byte field containing the list of permissible values if the return code is P. Figures 11.3A and 11.3B summarize this parameter.

Figure 11.3A Structure of Second Choice Exit Program Parameter if Code = C

Position	
1 - 30	Choice Text

Figure 11.3B Structure of Second Choice Exit Program Parameter if Code = P

Position	
1 - 2	Binary Value of number of entries
3 - 2000	List of permissible values

The first two bytes of the 2000-byte list of permissible values must contain the binary value of the number of entries in the list. Within the list, each entry consists of a 2-byte binary value describing the length of the entry (up to 32 characters long), followed by the entry itself.

Application Example

You have total control over what is in each entry. For example, Figure 11.4 shows a screen that appears when you press F4 for the parameter for Warehouse. The choice exit program in this example simply retrieves all valid warehouse codes from the master file and displays them.

Figure 11.4 Permissible Values List Displayed on F4

```
                    Specify Value for Parameter WH

Type choice, press Enter.

Type . . . . . . . . . . . . . . . . :     CHARACTER
WAREHOUSE (for ABC Code) . . . . . . .     80

001
10
101
20
30
35
40
60
65
70
75
76
80

F3=Exit   F5=Refresh   F12=Cancel   F13=How to use this display   F24=More keys
```

Coding a Simple Choice Exit Program

Figure 11.5 shows the simple RPG choice exit program that generates the screen in this example. The program retrieves a list of possible warehouses from a warehouse description file and builds a parameter to return to the command.

The parameters passed to and from the program in the PLIST at line 2400 consist of CTLPRM (the 21-byte value passed from the command to the program) and CHCTXT (the up to 2000-byte value passed back to the command). CTLPRM, as shown in the data structure (lines 1100 - 1400), consists of the three individual fields that make up parameter 1, defined in Figure 11.2. The important field here is OPTION, which represents the return code of either C or P. CHCTXT, as shown in its data structure (lines 1500 - 1800), consists of either a 30-byte text field (TEXT) or a 2-byte binary value (X) and array (VAL). The array VAL (defined in line 900) contains the elements of the permissible list, while the 2-byte binary value (X) holds the number of elements in the list.

The mainline of the program performs two different functions, depending on the value of the OPTION field. If the OPTION field is P, the user requested a list of permissible values (by pressing F4). The DO group in lines 3100 through 4000 reads the file containing the warehouse codes and loads the array VAL with the elements described by data structure VALUES (line 3900). Each element consists of a 2-byte binary prefix containing the length of the element, and the 3-character field containing the warehouse number.

When the OPTION field is C, the program performs the other function — to determine the choice text. This text is a literal that is simply moved to the field TEXT in line 4500.

Figure 11.5 RPG Choice Exit Program for Warehouse

```
     +... 1 ...+... 2 ...+... 3 ...+... 4 ...+... 5 ...+... 6 ...+... 7
 100 F*
 200 F* CHOICE PROGRAM FOR COMMANDS
 300 F* SENDS LISTS OF PERMISSIBLE VALUES FOR WAREHOUSE
 400 F*
 500 F*
 600 FIC170ML5IF  E         K              DISK
 700 E*******************************************************
 800 E                      TXT        1   1 30
 900 E                      VAL           99  5
1000 I*******************************************************
1100 ICTLPRM     DS
1200 I                                     1  10 CMD
1300 I                                    11  20 KWD
1400 I                                    21  21 OPTION
1500 ICHCTXT     DS                         2000
1600 I                                  B   1  20X
1700 I                                      3 497 VAL
1800 I                                      1  30 TEXT
1900 IVALUES     DS
2000 I                                  B   1  20VALLEN
2100 I                                      3   5 VALUE
2200 C*******************************************************
2300 C* PASSED PARMS
```

Figure 11.5 RPG Choice Exit Program for Warehouse, continued

```
      +... 1 ...+... 2 ...+... 3 ...+... 4 ...+... 5 ...+... 6 ...+... 7
2400 C              *ENTRY    PLIST
2500 C                        PARM                CTLPRM
2600 C                        PARM                CHCTXT
2700 C*
2800 C* PERMISSIBLE VALUES REQUESTED (USER PROMPTED WITH F4)
2900 C              OPTION    IFEQ 'P'
3000 C* LOAD ARRAY WITH VALID WAREHOUSE CODES
3100 C                        DO   99        X
3200 C*
3300 C                        READ IC170ML5                    90
3400 C              *IN90     IFEQ *ON
3500 C                        LEAVE
3600 C                        ENDIF
3700 C                        MOVELWDWHNO    VALUE
3800 C                        Z-ADD3         VALLEN
3900 C                        MOVE VALUES    VAL,X
4000 C                        ENDDO
4100 C*
4200 C                        ENDIF
4300 C* CHOICE TEXT REQUESTED
4400 C              OPTION    IFEQ 'C'
4500 C                        MOVELTXT,1     TEXT
4600 C                        ENDIF
4700 C                        MOVE *ON       *INLR
4800 C***************************************************************
** TEXT
Value, or F4 for list
```

Adding Descriptive Fields for Display

Because each entry in the list may be up to 32 characters long, it is frequently possible to show not only the values of the parameter (such as warehouse number), but also the description (such as warehouse name). Figure 11.6 shows the same choice exit program presented in Figure 11.5, but with the additional function of using the warehouse description in addition to the number.

We've made only a few changes to the second version of the program. Each entry in the VAL array (which will be passed back to the command to provide the list of permissible values) has been increased from 5 (2-byte binary field plus 3 bytes of data) to 25 (2-byte binary field plus 23 bytes of data). This change shows up in the array definition on line 900 and in the data structure on line 1700. The DO statement on line 3100 now checks for 50 iterations instead of 99. Line 3700, which builds each entry of the list, now concatenates the warehouse number to the warehouse name, giving a more complete description of each warehouse.

Figure 11.6 Choice Exit Program Using Code and Description

```
      +... 1 ...+... 2 ...+... 3 ...+... 4 ...+... 5 ...+... 6 ...+... 7
 100 F*
 200 F* CHOICE PROGRAM FOR COMMANDS
 300 F* SENDS LISTS OF PERMISSIBLE VALUES FOR WAREHOUSE
 400 F*
 500 F*
 600 FIC170ML5IF  E           K         DISK
 700 E*********************************************************
 800 E                    TXT    1   1 30
 900 E                    VAL        50 25
1000 I*********************************************************
1100 ICTLPRM      DS
1200 I                                     1  10 CMD
1300 I                                    11  20 KWD
1400 I                                    21  21 OPTION
1500 ICHCTXT      DS                         2000
1600 I                                 B   1  20X
1700 I                                    31252 VAL
1800 I                                     1  30 TEXT
1900 IVALUES      DS
2000 I                                 B   1  20VALLEN
2100 I                                     3  25 VALUE
2200 C*********************************************************
2300 C* PASSED PARMS
2400 C           *ENTRY    PLIST
2500 C                     PARM           CTLPRM
2600 C                     PARM           CHCTXT
2700 C*
2800 C* PERMISSIBLE VALUES REQUESTED (USER PROMPTED WITH F4)
2900 C           OPTION    IFEQ 'P'
3000 C* LOAD ARRAY WITH VALID WAREHOUSE CODES
3100 C                     DO   50        X
3200 C*
3300 C                     READ IC170ML5                 90
3400 C           *IN90     IFEQ *ON
3500 C                     LEAVE
3600 C                     ENDIF
3700 C           WDWHNO    CAT  WDWNAM:1   VALUE      P
3800 C                     Z-ADD23        VALLEN
3900 C                     MOVE VALUES    VAL,X
4000 C                     ENDDO
4100 C*
4200 C                     ENDIF
4300 C* CHOICE TEXT REQUESTED
4400 C           OPTION    IFEQ 'C'
4500 C                     MOVELTXT,1     TEXT
4600 C                     ENDIF
4700 C                     MOVE *ON       *INLR
4800
C*********************************************************
** TEXT
Value, or F4 for list
```

Figure 11.7 shows the results of this change.

Figure 11.7 Permissible Values with Description

```
                        Specify Value for Parameter WH

 Type choice, press Enter.

 Type . . . . . . . . . . . . . . . . :   CHARACTER
 WAREHOUSE (for ABC Code) . . . . . . .   80_


 001 DANAHER TOOL GROUP
 10 DTG FAYETTEVILLE
 101 IN TRANSIT WAREHOUS
 20 LANCASTER LITERATURE
 30 K-D TOOLS OF CANADA
 35 K-D INTERNATIONAL
 40 JACOBS CHUCK CLEMSON
 60 DTG - SPRINGDALE
 65 DTG - GASTONIA
 70 DTG - SPRINGFIELD
 75 HOLOKROME W HARTFORD
 76 PTD - WEST ORANGE
 80 PTD - BALTIMORE


 F3=Exit   F5=Refresh   F12=Cancel   F13=How to use this display   F24=More keys
```

Because the list of permissible values is limited to 2000 bytes, you will use a choice exit program only to retrieve a list containing a finite number of values, such as state codes. You will never use it for a list that can contain an almost unlimited number of values, such as item numbers.

Validity-Checking Programs

Chapter 12

Use a validity-checking program to perform editing that you cannot do using command definition statements.

Commands provide extensive editing functions through various PARM statement keywords such as TYPE and VALUES, and through the DEP statement. Sometimes, however, you need to perform additional editing, such as comparing entered values against data in a file. A validity-checking program gives you this capability.

A validity-checking program is a program (written in any language) that performs any type of editing for a command. The validity-checking program is associated with the command when you execute CRTCMD to compile the program, as shown in Figure 12.1.

Figure 12.1 CRTCMD Command Specifying a Validity-Checking Program

```
                        Create Command (CRTCMD)

 Type choices, press Enter.

 Command . . . . . . . . . . . .   SARPTCMD      Name
   Library . . . . . . . . . . .     *CURLIB     Name, *CURLIB
 Program to process command. . .   SARPTC        Name, *REXX
   Library . . . . . . . . . . .     *LIBL       Name, *LIBL, *CURLIB
 Source file . . . . . . . . . .   QCMDSRC       Name
   Library . . . . . . . . . . .     *LIBL       Name, *LIBL, *CURLIB
 Source member . . . . . . . . .   *CMD          Name, *CMD
 Text 'description'. . . . . . .   *SRCMBRTXT

 Additional Parameters

 Validity checking program . . .   SARPTVC       Name, *NONE
   Library . . . . . . . . . . .     *CURLIB     Name, *LIBL, *CURLIB
 Mode in which valid . . . . . .   *ALL          *ALL, *PROD, *DEBUG, *SERVICE
                 + for more values
                                                                    More...
 F3=Exit   F4=Prompt   F5=Refresh   F12=Cancel   F13=How to use this display
 F24=More keys
```

When you have specified a validity-checking program, the command passes all parameters to that program when the user presses Enter. You code the validity-checking program to perform the appropriate editing and send diagnostic and escape messages back to the previous call level (the command) if any errors occur. These messages then appear on the command prompt screen. You write the validity-checking program, issue the messages, and name the program when you create the command, using the CRTCMD command. All the rest of the function is automatic. The messages you use for validity checking can be in a message file, or you can use the generic message identifier, CPD0006.

Validity-Checking Program with CPD0006

Validity-checking programs can use the generic CPD0006 message to return error messages.

Our first example uses the generic message CPD0006. IBM has reserved this message ID for our use. To use this facility, you simply issue MSGID CPD0006 and supply the data for the message right in your program. This dynamic use of messages is a good choice when your messages are specific to the program and will not be used by other programs.

Coding the Validity-Checking Program

The CL program in Figure 12.2 edits three parameters. For two of the edits (QUOTE and WH), the program calls an RPG program that edits the data and passes an error parameter back to the CL program. The other parameter (OUTQ) is edited in the CL program. If either the RPG or the CL program detects an error, the CL program issues message CPD0006, with the appropriate text and values substituted. Finally, if any errors are detected, escape message CPF0002 returns control to the calling level and the error message appears. Figure 12.2 shows the CL program that we specified as the validity-checking program in the CRTCMD command.

Figure 12.2 Validity-Checking Program Using CPD0006

```
            PGM         PARM(&QUOTE &SORT &REQUESTER &OUTQ &COPIES &WH)
/* DECLARE VARIABLES */
            DCL         VAR(&QUOTE) TYPE(*CHAR) LEN(6)
            DCL         VAR(&SORT) TYPE(*CHAR) LEN(1)
            DCL         VAR(&OUTQ) TYPE(*CHAR) LEN(10)
            DCL         VAR(&REQUESTER) TYPE(*CHAR) LEN(10)
            DCL         VAR(&COPIES) TYPE(*CHAR) LEN(2)
            DCL         VAR(&WH) TYPE(*CHAR) LEN(3)
            DCL         VAR(&ERROR) TYPE(*CHAR) LEN(1)
            DCL         VAR(&QTERR) TYPE(*CHAR) LEN(1)
            DCL         VAR(&WHERR) TYPE(*CHAR) LEN(1)
/* CHECK QUOTE FOR VALIDITY */
            CALL        PGM(QUOTEVC) PARM(&QUOTE &QTERR)
            IF          COND(&QTERR *EQ 'Y') THEN(DO)
            SNDPGMMSG   MSGID(CPD0006) MSGF(QCPFMSG) MSGDTA('0000 +
                          Quote Number is Invalid') MSGTYPE(*DIAG)
            CHGVAR      VAR(&ERROR) VALUE('Y')
```

Figure 12.2 Validity-Checking Program Using CPD0006, continued

```
                    ENDDO
/* CHECK OUTQ FOR VALIDITY */
                    CHKOBJ    OBJ(&OUTQ) OBJTYPE(*OUTQ)
                    MONMSG    MSGID(CPF9801) EXEC(DO)
                    SNDPGMMSG MSGID(CPD0006) MSGF(QCPFMSG) MSGDTA('0000 +
                                Printer Output Queue is Invalid') +
                                MSGTYPE(*DIAG)
                    CHGVAR    VAR(&ERROR) VALUE('Y')
                    ENDDO
/* CHECK WH FOR VALIDITY */
                    IF        COND(&WH *NE ' ') THEN(DO)
                    CALL      PGM(WHVC) PARM(&WH &WHERR)
                    IF        COND(&WHERR *EQ 'Y') THEN(DO)
                    SNDPGMMSG MSGID(CPD0006) MSGF(QCPFMSG) MSGDTA('0000 +
                                Warehouse is Invalid ') MSGTYPE(*DIAG)
                    CHGVAR    VAR(&ERROR) VALUE('Y')
                    ENDDO
                    ENDDO
/* IF ANY ERRORS, SEND ESCAPE MESSAGE */
                    IF        COND(&ERROR *EQ 'Y') THEN(SNDPGMMSG +
                                MSGID(CPF0002) MSGF(QCPFMSG) +
                                MSGTYPE(*ESCAPE))
                    ENDPGM
```

Notice the three SNDPGMMSG commands that specify MSGID CPD0006. In each case, the edit program has identified an error. We send a message, using CPD0006 from message file QCPFMSG, and then we include the message text right in the command. All these messages are set up as diagnostic messages.

Error Messages

Figure 12.3 shows the command prompt screen after the error messages have been sent and control has been returned. Note the error message at the bottom of the screen.

The validity-checking program sends escape message CPF0002 to allow the user to correct errors.

If the validity-checking program finds any errors and issues escape message CPF0002, the command will redisplay the prompt screen for the user to correct the errors. This loop will continue until the user corrects all errors. When we get a clean run through the validity-checking program, with no errors, the command will pass control to the CPP.

```
                      Monthly Sales Report (SARPTCMD)

 Type choices, press Enter.

   Fiscal Period . . . . . . . . .   1294        MMYY
   Requester . . . . . . . . . . .   BOBSMITH
   Printer Output Queue . . . . . .  QWERTY        Printer Output Queue
   Number of Copies . . . . . . . .  1




                                                            Bottom
   F3=Exit   F4=Prompt   F5=Refresh   F12=Cancel   F13=How to use this display
   F24=More keys
   Printer Output Group is Invalid
```

Validity-Checking Program with a Message File

Create a message file to set up messages that validity-checking programs will use.

If you will be using general messages, you probably will want to use a message file to send error messages back to the command. By using a message file, you can set up messages that multiple programs can use.

Creating Messages

The first task is to use ADDMSGD to create the messages you will need, as shown in Figure 12.4. This example will check for a valid printer output queue, so the message needs to alert the users when they have entered an invalid printer output queue. When adding the message, you must specify the message identifier and the first-level message text. You may optionally include a more detailed description in the second-level message text. This text is displayed if help is requested on the first-level message text.

Validity-checking programs require at least one message data field, 4 characters containing 0000.

You must also specify at least one message data-field format (available on the second screen of the prompted ADDMSGD command, as shown in Figure 12.5), which the system uses internally. This format is a 4-byte character field and should always be 0000. In our example, we are using a second message data-field format to pass the invalid value for the field being edited (in this case, printer output queue) back to the command so that it can be displayed in the message.

Figure 12.4 Creating a Message in a Message File (Screen 1 of 2)

```
                    Add Message Description (ADDMSGD)

 Type choices, press Enter.

   Message identifier . . . . . . .   msg0098      Name
   Message file . . . . . . . . . .   samsg        Name
     Library. . . . . . . . . . . .   *LIBL        Name, *LIBL, *CURLIB
   First-level message text . . . .   Printer Outq &2 is not valid


 _____
   Second-level message text . . . .  *NONE
 _____
 _____
 _____
 _____
 _____
 _____
 _____   ...
   Severity code . . . . . . . . . .  00           0-99


                                                                   More...
 F3=Exit   F4=Prompt   F5=Refresh   F10=Additional parameters   F12=Cancel
 F13=How to use this display        F24=More keys
```

Figure 12.5 Creating a Message in a Message File (Screen 2 of 2)

```
                  Specify More Values for Parameter FMT

 Type choices, press Enter.

 Message data fields formats:
   Data type. . . . . . . . . . .   *CHAR        *NONE, *QTDCHAR, *CHAR...
   Length . . . . . . . . . . . .   4            Number, *VARY
   *VARY bytes or dec pos . . . .   0            Number

   Data type. . . . . . . . . . .   *CHAR        *QTDCHAR, *CHAR, *HEX...
   Length . . . . . . . . . . . .   10           Number, *VARY
   *VARY bytes or dec pos . . . .   0            Number

   Data type. . . . . . . . . . .                *QTDCHAR, *CHAR, *HEX...
   Length . . . . . . . . . . . .   *VARY        Number, *VARY
   *VARY bytes or dec pos . . . .   0            Number

   Data type. . . . . . . . . . .                *QTDCHAR, *CHAR, *HEX...
   Length . . . . . . . . . . . .   *VARY        Number, *VARY
   *VARY bytes or dec pos . . . .   0            Number
                                                                   More...
 F3=Exit   F4=Prompt   F5=Refresh   F12=Cancel   F13=How to use this display
 F24=More keys
```

Notice that in our first-level message text, we used the variable &2. Because we have defined our message data-field format in the second position, we will use the variable &2 to refer to it. This value is substituted in the actual message text for the variable &2 when it is displayed, as shown in Figure 12.6. (If you need more information about message handling, see IBM's manual, *CL Programming* (SC41-3721).

The validity-checking program processes the command parameters and sends the messages back to the command. All error messages are sent as diagnostic messages; then a single escape message, CPF0002, is sent. The result is the same as when we use the generic message ID technique.

Figure 12.6 Prompt Screen with Error Message from Validity-Checking Program

```
                        Monthly Sales Report (SARPTCMD)

 Type choices, press Enter.

 Fiscal Period . . . . . . . . .  1294         MMYY
 Requester . . . . . . . . . . .  BOBSMITH_
 Printer Output Queue . . . . . .  QWERTY____   Printer Output Queue
 Number of Copies . . . . . . . .  1_




                                                                    Bottom
 F3=Exit    F4=Prompt   F5=Refresh   F12=Cancel   F13=How to use this display
 F24=More keys
 Printer Outq QWERTY is Invalid
```

Coding the Validity-Checking Program

A portion of the validity-checking program for this example is shown in Figure 12.7. This CL program checks the value of the passed parameter &OUTQ for validity. If &OUTQ is invalid, the program sends a message with the appropriate message identifier. The program passes the value of the invalid printer output queue in the MSGDTA parameter (concatenated to the required 0000 value of the first message data-field format). Notice that the message is sent as a diagnostic message. Finally, if any errors are found, the validity-checking program sends escape message CPF0002, which returns control to the calling level and displays the message.

Figure 12.7 Validity-Checking CL Program for Testing OUTQ

```
            PGM         PARM(&WKMMYY &RQSTR &OUTQ &COPIES)
/* DECLARE VARIABLES */
            DCL         VAR(&WKMMYY) TYPE(*CHAR) LEN(4)
            DCL         VAR(&RQSTR) TYPE(*CHAR) LEN(10)
            DCL         VAR(&OUTQ) TYPE(*CHAR) LEN(10)
            DCL         VAR(&COPIES) TYPE(*CHAR) LEN(2)
            DCL         VAR(&ERROR) TYPE(*CHAR) LEN(1)
/* CHECK OUTQ FOR VALIDITY */
            CHKOBJ      OBJ(&OUTQ) OBJTYPE(*OUTQ)
            MONMSG      MSGID(CPF9801) EXEC(DO)
            SNDPGMMSG   MSGID(MSG0099) MSGF(SAMSG) +
                          MSGDTA('0000'||&OUTQ) MSGTYPE(*DIAG)
            CHGVAR      VAR(&ERROR) VALUE('Y')
            ENDDO
/* IF ANY ERRORS, SEND ESCAPE MESSAGE */
            IF          COND(&ERROR *EQ 'Y') THEN(SNDPGMMSG +
                          MSGID(CPF0002) MSGF(QCPFMSG) +
                          MSGTYPE(*ESCAPE))

            ENDPGM
```

For the most efficiency, you can write a single validity-checking program to validate many commands. You use the CONSTANT keyword of the PARM statement as a place holder. Chapter 8 covered this concept.

Prompt-Override Programs

Chapter 13

Use prompt-override programs to assign variable default values to a command parameter.

You have seen how to assign default values to command parameters by using the DFT keyword on the PARM statement. This works fine when the default is a known constant, but what do you do when the default value that you want to use is a variable that can change or can even be different for each user? For example, how can you specify a user's current output queue value as the default printer output queue? The answer is to use a prompt-override program.

Prompt-Override Program Example

A prompt-override program retrieves current parameter values that the command will then display as the default. IBM uses prompt-override programs frequently. For example, when you use the CHGUSRPRF (Change User Profile) command, the system displays the screen shown in Figure 13.1. After you enter a user profile name and press Enter, the system displays the current values for the specified user profile name in many of the parameters (Figure 13.2). Some parameters whose values are retrieved are user class, current library, initial program, and text description.

Figure 13.1 CHGUSRPRF Command Prompt Screen

```
                        Change User Profile (CHGUSRPRF)

 Type choices, press Enter.

 User profile . . . . . . . . . . LAN_____       Name






                                                                    Bottom
 F3=Exit   F4=Prompt   F5=Refresh   F10=Additional parameters   F12=Cancel
 F13=How to use this display        F24=More keys
```

Figure 13.2 CHGUSRPRF Command with Retrieved Values

```
                        Change User Profile (CHGUSRPRF)

 Type choices, press Enter.

 User profile . . . . . . . . . .     LAN_____     Name
 User password. . . . . . . . . .     *SAME_____    Name, *SAME, *NONE
 Set password to expired. . . . .     *NO___        *SAME, *NO, *YES
 Status . . . . . . . . . . . . .     *ENABLED_     *SAME, *ENABLED, *DISABLED
 User class . . . . . . . . . . .     *PGMR___      *SAME, *USER, *SYSOPR...
 Assistance level . . . . . . . .     *ADVANCED     *SAME, *SYSVAL, *BASIC...
 Current library. . . . . . . . .     *CRTDFT       Name, *SAME, *CRTDFT
 Initial program to call. . . . .     INITPGMR_     Name, *S
   Library. . . . . . . . . . . .      UTILS___     Name, *LIBL, *CURLIB
 Limit capabilities . . . . . . .     *NO___        *SAME, *NO, *PARTIAL, *YES
 Text 'description' . . . . . . .     'lynn_nelson_profile'_____



                                                                    Bottom
 F3=Exit   F4=Prompt   F5=Refresh   F10=Additional parameters   F12=Cancel
 F13=How to use this display        F24=More keys
```

Steps to Use Prompt Override

Use KEYPARM(*YES) to identify key parameters in a command.

You can use this technique with your own custom commands. Using a prompt-override program involves three steps. First, you must identify the key parameter(s). Key parameters are those that uniquely identify the parameters to retrieve. In the last example, the user profile name is the key parameter because its value is needed to retrieve the values of the other user profile parameters. You define the key parameters in the command source by specifying KEYPARM(*YES) on the PARM statement. You must specify all key parameters first in the command, before the other PARMs.

The second step to use a prompt-override program is to write the program that will retrieve the values. This program can be in any programming language. You can have only one prompt-override program per command.

Finally, when compiling the command with the CRTCMD command, you specify your prompt-override program name, as shown in Figure 13.3. These prompts occur on the second page of the Additional Parameters on the Create Command (CRTCMD) prompt screen.

Figure 13.3 CRTCMD Specifying a Prompt-Override Program

```
                          Create Command (CRTCMD)

 Type choices, press Enter.

 Prompt override program . . . .    POPPGM        Name, *NONE
   Library . . . . . . . . . .       *CURLIB      Name, *LIBL, *CURLIB
 Authority . . . . . . . . . .      *LIBCRTAUT    Name, *LIBCRTAUT, *USE...
 Replace command . . . . . . .      *YES          *YES, *NO








                                                                   Bottom
 F3=Exit   F4=Prompt    F5=Refresh    F12=Cancel   F13=How to use this display
 F24=More keys
```

Custom Command Example

The following custom command example, CHGOUTQ (Change Default OUTQ), lets you change a user's default OUTQ. Let's begin with the command source for the command. Following is the source for this simple command:

```
CMD        PROMPT('Change Default Output Queue')
PARM       KWD(USRPRF) TYPE(*CHAR) LEN(10) MIN(1) +
             KEYPARM(*YES) PROMPT('User Profile')
PARM       KWD(OUTQ) TYPE(*NAME) DFT(*SAME) +
             CHOICE(*NONE) PROMPT('Output Queue')
```

Notice that the first PARM, USRPRF, has KEYPARM(*YES) specified. This identifies the USRPRF PARM as the key parameter, the one used to retrieve values with the prompt-override program.

In this example, the prompt-override program retrieves the current default output queue of the selected user profile and passes the values back to the command, where its name will then be displayed.

The command must first prompt the user for the user profile to be changed. The keyword KEYPARM(*YES) tells the command which parameter the prompt-override program will need to retrieve the necessary information. When you code a command with prompt override, the prompting process is in two steps. The command first prompts all the PARMs that have KEYPARM(*YES) specified. That information is then passed to the prompt-override program so that it can retrieve the necessary information. When the prompt-override program has completed, it sends the retrieved information back to the command, which then displays the second half of the prompt with any information sent from the prompt-override program. Figures 13.4 and 13.5 show this two-step process.

Figure 13.4 CHGOUTQ Command Prompt Screen

```
                 Change Default Output Queue (CHGOUTQCMD)

Type choices, press Enter.

User Profile . . . . . . . . .   LAN            Character value












                                                              Bottom
F3=Exit   F4=Prompt   F5=Refresh   F12=Cancel   F13=How to use this display
F24=More keys
```

Figure 13.5 CHGOUTQ Command Showing Retrieved Value

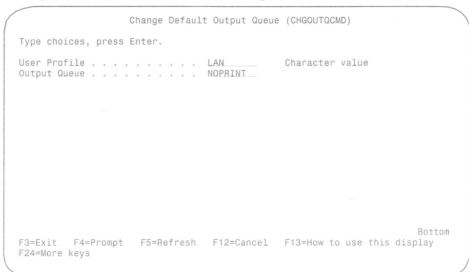

```
                    Change Default Output Queue (CHGOUTQCMD)

 Type choices, press Enter.

 User Profile . . . . . . . . . .   LAN_____        Character value
 Output Queue . . . . . . . . . .   NOPRINT_




                                                                    Bottom
 F3=Exit   F4=Prompt   F5=Refresh   F12=Cancel   F13=How to use this display
 F24=More keys
```

Prompt-Override Parameters

Three groups of parameters are passed between the command and the prompt-override program, as summarized in Figure 13.6. The first parameter (20 bytes long) contains the qualified command name. This parameter will tell the prompt-override program which command is sending it information. This gives you the potential to code one prompt-override program that different commands can use.

The second group of one or more parameters, also passed from the command to the prompt-override program, contains the key parameter(s) values. Because you can have more than one key parameter and the key parameters can be of any size, the number of parameters in this group will vary from command to command. In our CHGOUTQ example, the user profile parameter results in a single key parameter of 10 characters.

Figure 13.6 Summary of Parameters for Prompt-Override Programs

Prompt-Override Parameters		
First Parameter		
	Command Name	10
	Library Name	10
Middle Group of Parameters		
	Key Parm(s) values	variable lengths
Final Parameter		
	Length of string	2
	String with retrieved values	5698

The final parameter is passed from the prompt-override program back to the command. This single parameter is a 5700-byte string containing the retrieved values. The first two bytes of this string will contain the length (in binary) of the string that is returned.

The string to be returned to the command must use the keyword format to pass the retrieved values back to the command. Keyword format means that for each value returned, you must first specify the keyword (KWD from the command PARM statement) and then put the value for that keyword in parentheses. This specification lets the command determine what values to display in which parameters. The following code example is in keyword format:

```
OUTQ(QPRINT)
```

This string tells the command to put the value QPRINT into the parameter for the keyword OUTQ.

In addition to the keyword and parameter value, you must also include selective prompt characters in the return string to tell the command how to display each parameter. This is one of those "do it because IBM told you to" rules. Always add a ?? before each keyword so that the command will prompt the parameter. If you take the OUTQ example, your return string for OUTQ looks like the following string:

```
??OUTQ(QPRINT)
```

The first two bytes of this up-to-5700-character string represent the binary value of the number of characters in the entire string. Our example has a total of 18 — 2 bytes for the ?? prompting characters, 4 bytes for the keyword **OUTQ**, 2 bytes for the parentheses, and 10 bytes for the value of the OUTQ parameter. Even though the value we retrieved (QPRINT) has only 6 characters, we have a potential for a longer value, so we include the maximum of 10 in our calculations. The final layout of the string that returns a value of QPRINT to the command for the OUTQ PARM of the CHGOUTQ command will look like the following sample (note that the 0018 will be in binary format):

$^0_0{}^1_8$??OUTQ(QPRINT)

The CL prompt-override program for CHGOUTQ is shown in the code that follows. This simple program retrieves the current default OUTQ value of the selected user profile and formats it appropriately into the 5700-character string.

```
PGM         PARM(&CMD &USRPRF &STRING)
/* DECLARE VARIABLES */
            DCL      VAR(&CMD) TYPE(*CHAR) LEN(20)
            DCL      VAR(&USRPRF) TYPE(*CHAR) LEN(10)
            DCL      VAR(&STRING) TYPE(*CHAR) LEN(5700)
            DCL      VAR(&KWD) TYPE(*CHAR) LEN(7) VALUE('??OUTQ(')
            DCL      VAR(&OUTQ) TYPE(*CHAR) LEN(10)
            DCL      VAR(&DECLEN) TYPE(*DEC) LEN(5 0) VALUE(18)
            DCL      VAR(&BINLEN) TYPE(*CHAR) LEN(2)

/* RETRIEVE CURRENT DEFAULT OUTQ */
            RTVUSRPRF USRPRF(&USRPRF) OUTQ(&OUTQ)

/* FORMAT STRING VARIABLE */
            CHGVAR   (%BIN(&BINLEN)) VALUE(&DECLEN)
            CHGVAR   VAR(&STRING) VALUE(&BINLEN)
            CHGVAR   VAR(&STRING) VALUE(&STRING *TCAT &KWD)
            CHGVAR   VAR(&STRING) VALUE(&STRING *TCAT &OUTQ)
            CHGVAR   VAR(&STRING) VALUE(&STRING *TCAT ')')

            ENDPGM
```

As a review, the first parameter (&CMD) contains the command and library of the calling command (i.e., CHGOUTQ LANLIB). The second parameter (&USRPRF) is used to retrieve the user profile and gets the default output queue. This parameter contains the value of the PARMs that have been coded with KEYPARM(*YES) (i.e., LAN). The third parameter (&STRING) will contain the information that the prompt-override program has retrieved and is returning to the command (i.e., $^0_0{}^1_8$??OUTQ(NOPRINT)).

Summary of Steps for Using Prompt-Override Programs

1. Specify KEYPARM(*YES) on key parameters in the command source.
2. Write the prompt-override program.
3. Specify the prompt-override program when compiling the command.

Online Help

Chapter 14

All IBM-supplied commands provide online help. With the press of a key, users can retrieve and view information to assist them in entering values into the command. You can also get online help with user-written commands. Using online help with your own commands increases the user-friendliness of your applications and improves both your productivity and that of your users.

User Interface Manager

To provide help with your commands, use User Interface Manager (UIM) panel groups.

The only way to provide online help with commands is with the User Interface Manager (UIM) utility. IBM uses UIM to create its menus, help panels, screen lists, and so on. UIM is a complex, powerful product that is beyond the scope of this book. We will, however, provide a simple UIM help example to get you started. For additional information, see IBM's *Application Display Programming* manual (SC41-3715).

UIM uses objects called panel groups (type *PNLGRP) to store the help text and the code for the help function. The panel group defines how the text will appear on the screen and how it will function. UIM help text information is coded into a source member (type PNLGRP) and then compiled into a panel group object using the CRTPNLGRP (Create Panel Group) command.

UIM is a tag-based language. Tags are the statements used to code a panel group. There are dozens of different kinds of tag statements, but coding help text for a command requires using only a few of them.

You take two steps to incorporate online help into your commands. First, you must create the help text in a UIM help panel group. Then, when creating the command with CRTCMD, you specify the help panel and help identifier, as shown in Figure 14.1.

Figure 14.1 CRTCMD Specifying Help Panels

```
                          Create Command (CRTCMD)

 Type choices, press Enter.

 Where allowed to run. . . . . . .  *ALL          *ALL, *BATCH, *INTERACT...
                   + for more values
 Allow limited users . . . . . . .  *NO           *NO, *YES
 Maximum positional parameters . .  *NOMAX        0-75, *NOMAX
 Message file for prompt text. . .  *NONE         Name, *NONE
   Library . . . . . . . . . . . .                Name, *LIBL, *CURLIB
 Message file. . . . . . . . . . .  QCPFMSG       Name
   Library . . . . . . . . . . . .     *LIBL      Name, *LIBL, *CURLIB
 Help panel group. . . . . . . . .  sarpthlp      Name, *NONE
   Library . . . . . . . . . . . .                Name, *LIBL, *CURLIB
 Help identifier . . . . . . . . .  sarpthlp      Character value, *CMD, *NONE
 Help search index . . . . . . . .  *NONE         Name, *NONE, *SYSTEM
   Library . . . . . . . . . . . .                Name, *LIBL, *CURLIB
 Current library . . . . . . . . .  *NOCHG        Name, *NOCHG, *CRTDFT
 Product library . . . . . . . . .  *NOCHG        Name, *NOCHG, *NONE


                                                           More...
 F3=Exit   F4=Prompt   F12=Cancel   F13=How to use this display
 F24=More keys
```

Panel Group Source Member

To create the UIM help panel, create a source member (type PNLGRP). The standard source file name for UIM members is QPNLSRC. This member is where you will enter the help text and tag statements. Here is an example:

```
:pnlgrp.
:help name=sarpthlp.
Monthly Sales Report - Help
:p.
This screen allows the Monthly Sales Report to run. You
may specify the information required to run this report.
:ehelp.
:help name='sarpthlp/wkreq'.
Requester
:xh3.Requester
:p.
This is where you specify the name of the person to
receive the report. This value will print in the heading
of the report.
:ehelp.
:help name='sarpthlp/wkcopy'.
Number of Copies
:xh3.Number of Copies
:p.
Specify the number of copies of the report to print. Valid
values are between 1 and 99.
```

```
:ehelp.
:help name='sarpthlp/wkoutq'.
Printer Output Queue
:xh3.Printer Output Queue
:p.
Specify which printer output queue is to print the report.
For a list of valid printer output queues, press F4.
:ehelp.
```

The :pnlgrp and :epnlgrp tags mark the boundaries of a panel group.

This code sample uses four different tag statements. Tag statements always begin with a colon. The first (and mandatory) tag statement is the **:pnlgrp** tag. This statement identifies the begining of the panel group (only one is allowed). The **:pnlgrp** tag has a matching **:epnlgrp** (end panel group) tag that identifies the end of the panel group.

Help text for each help module appears between :help and :ehelp tags.

The **:help** tag identifies the beginning of a help module, while its corresponding **:ehelp** tag identifies the end of the group. The help text for the help module appears between the **:help** and **:ehelp** tags. The name value on the **:help** tag refers to the help identifier specified when you compile the command. You can also specify a command keyword for the parameter if this help text is specific to a parameter. The text for the help screen title appears immediately following the **:help** tag.

Paragraph tags (:p tags) identify new paragraphs.

The **:p** (paragraph) tag makes the help text easier to read by acting like a carriage return. It causes the text that follows the tag to appear on a new line.

Heading tags (:xh1, :xh2, :xh3, and :xh4) format different heading levels in the help text.

We have also used several **:xh3** tags in the preceding example to identify extended headings. Four extended heading levels are available, **:xh1** through **:xh4**. Each tag causes the heading to print in a slightly different format.

> **:xh1** Centered, underlined, and highlighted
>
> **:xh2** Left justified, underlined, and highlighted
>
> **:xh3** Left justified and highlighted
>
> **:xh4** Left justified and underlined

You can see the extended headings in Figure 14.3 on page 131.

The first **:help name** tag statement simply states the help identifier (no parameter names). This statement is used for extended help. The other qualified **:help name** tag statements specify the individual keywords for each parameter. For example, the help text for the parameter REQUESTER follows the tag, **:help name='sarpthlp/wkreq'**, where WKREQ is the keyword name for the parameter for requester.

After you create and compile the help panel source (and specify the appropriate help panel and identifier names when you create the command), the Help key will display cursor-sensitive text.

Figure 14.2 shows the result of pressing the Help key with the cursor in the Printer Output Queue parameter.

Figure 14.2 Cursor-Sensitive Help Text Displayed

```
                      Monthly Sales Report (MONSARPT)

Type choices, press Enter.
Requester. . . . . . . . . . .  _____   Your Name
Printer Output Queue . . . . . .   QPRINT__
Number of Cop ...................................................................
              :                 Printer Output Queue                          :
              :                                                                :
              : Specify which printer output queue is to print the report.    :
              : For a list of valid printer output queues, press F4.           :
              :                                                      Bottom    :
              : F2=Extended help   F3=Exit help       F10=Move to top          :
              : F12=Cancel         F13=User support   F14=Print help           :
              :                                                                :
              :                                                                :
              ..................................................................


                                                                     Bottom
F3=Exit   F4=Prompt   F5=Refresh   F12=Cancel   F13=How to use this display
F24=More keys
```

UIM Options

The user's default user option for help screens determines how the help is displayed (full screen or window). In this example, the user profile value for USROPT is not *HLPFUL, which causes the help text to be displayed in a window, not a full screen. If F2 is pressed for extended help, the system displays the screen shown in Figure 14.3. This screen shows the extended text (specified on the first **:help name** tag), followed by all help text for that help identifier.

Although using UIM to create online help text for commands at first seems tedious, once you become used to UIM's structure and syntax, you will find it easy. This simple example barely scratches the surface of what UIM offers for online help. Additional features, such as search index and hypertext, are available to make the help text for your commands as functional as IBM's.

Figure 14.3 Extended Help

```
                    Monthly Sales Report (MONSARPT)
.................................................................
:                  Monthly Sales Report - Help                  :
:                                                               :
:     This screen allows the Monthly Sales Report to run. You may specify  :
:     the information required to run this report.              :
:                                                               :
: Requester                                                     :
:                                                               :
:     This is where you specify the name of the person to receive the  :
:     report. This value will print in the heading of the report.  :
:                                                               :
: Printer Output Queue                                          :
:                                                               :
:     Specify which printer output queue is to print the report. For a  :
:     list of valid printer output queues, press F4.           :
:                                                               :
: Number of Copies                                              :
:                                                               :
:                                                  More...      :
:                                                               :
: F3=Exit help    F10=Move to top    F12=Cancel    F13=User support  :
: F14=Print help                                                :
:                                                               :
:.................................................................:
```

Section 4

Appendices

Summary of Command Definition Statements

Appendix A

Command Definition Statements	
CMD	The Command statement is the only mandatory command definition statement. It provides the title text that appears on the command prompt screen.
PARM	The purpose of this powerful statement is to define parameters. PARM is used to set up simple lists, perform editing, display choices, and more.
ELEM	The Element statement is used to create mixed lists (a set of separately defined elements for a single parameter).
QUAL	The Qualifier statement defines qualified name parameters.
PMTCTL	The Prompt Control statement is used to condition the presentation of parameters on the values of other parameters.
DEP	The Dependency statement enforces relationships between parameters.

Parameter Types

Appendix B

This table describes a dozen commonly used parameter types. The parameter types not listed in this table occur mainly in IBM-supplied commands. You use all these parameter types on both the PARM and ELEM statements. With the exception of *DEC, *DATE, *TIME, *LGL, and *HEX, you may also use them on the QUAL statements.

Parameter Types	
*CHAR	A character string (up to 3000 characters).
*DEC	A packed-decimal number.
*DATE	A character string that is a valid date. *DATE is passed to the CPP as CYYMMDD.
*TIME	A 6-character string that is a valid time. *TIME is passed to the CPP as HHMMSS.
*NAME	A character string that is a valid system name (up to 256 characters). The first character must be A-Z, $, @, or #. The remaining characters may be A-Z, $, @, #, 0-9, "_", and ".".
*SNAME	A character string that is the same as *NAME, except that periods are not allowed.
*CNAME	A character string that is the same as *NAME, except that periods and underscores are not allowed.
*GENERIC	A character string (up to 256 bytes) with the last character being an asterisk. Used as a wild-card designation.
*LGL	A logical value of either 1 or 0.
*HEX	The value is converted to hexadecimal characters.
*INT2	The value is a 2-byte binary integer.
*INT4	The value is a 4-byte binary integer.

Summary of
PARM Statement Keywords

Appendix C

The following PARM statement keywords are the ones this book covers, plus a few others that you can use in custom-written commands. The keywords not covered in this table are for IBM-supplied commands.

PARM Statement Keywords		
KWD	Keyword	The PARM's field name for referencing PARMs within a command and with selective prompting.
TYPE	Type	A value that defines the PARM's attributes, such as character, decimal, and so on. (See Appendix B: Parameter Types.)
LEN	Length	A value that determines the length (and decimal positions, if decimal type) of the PARM.
CONSTANT	Constant	CONSTANT passes a fixed value from the command to the CPP. A PARM with a CONSTANT value is not displayed on the prompt screen. Can be used as a placeholder for dummy parameters. Also used to create single command macros without a CPP.
RSTD	Restricted	A value of *YES in this keyword restricts input to this PARM to the values specified on the VALUES, SPCVAL, and SNGVAL keywords.
DFT	Default	A default value that you assign to the PARM.

PARM Statement Keywords, continued		
VALUES	Values	This keyword specifies up to 300 values that are valid for the PARM. Used with RSTD(*YES).
REL	Relationship	This keyword enforces the specified relationship between the PARM and a constant, or between the PARM and another PARM.
RANGE	Range	A range of values that you specify as valid for the PARM.
SPCVAL	Special values	This keyword lets you specify up to 300 valid values that users can enter for the PARM. These values do not have to meet the PARM's validity requirements. This keyword can be used to translate an entered value to another value.
MIN	Minimum number of values	A value that defines the minimum number of values that a user may enter. MIN(1) is used to make a PARM mandatory.
MAX	Maximum number of values	A value that defines the maximum number of values that a user can enter. MAX is used to define a simple list.
FULL	Full entry	A value of *YES forces the number of characters entered for the PARM to be equal to the length of the PARM.
CHOICE	Choice text	This keyword specifies the CHOICE text that displays to the right of the input field. There are five options: 1. Up to 30 characters of fixed text. 2. *VALUES, which will display all possible values (based on DFT, SPCVAL, SNGVAL, Values, etc.). 3. A message identifier, used to retrieve the CHOICE text. 4. *PGM, to use a choice exit program to retrieve the choice text and permissible values list. 5. *NONE, to display no choice text.
PMTCTL	Prompt Control	A value that conditions the presentation of the PARM on F10 or on the value of other parameters.

PARM Statement Keywords, continued		
KEYPARM	Key Parameter	A value of *YES designates the PARM as the key parameter used by a prompt-override program to retrieve current values.
PROMPT	Prompt	This keyword specifies the prompt text, which displays to the left of the input field. Can be up to 30 characters if fixed text or a message identifier used to retrieve the prompt text. The PROMPT keyword can also determine the order in which parameters appear on the prompt screen if you specify an optional relative prompt number.

Summary of ELEM Statement Keywords

The ELEM statement defines parameters that are elements of a mixed list, so most of its keywords are identical to those of the PARM statement. This book covers the keywords in this table.

ELEM Statement Keywords		
TYPE	Type	A value that defines the element's attributes, such as character, decimal, and so on. (See Appendix B: Parameter Types.)
LEN	Length	A value that determines the length (and decimal positions, if decimal type) of the element.
CONSTANT	Constant	CONSTANT passes a fixed value from the command to the CPP. An element with a CONSTANT value is not displayed on the prompt screen. Can be used as a placeholder for dummy elements.
RSTD	Restricted	A value of *YES in this keyword restricts input to this element to the values specified on the VALUES, SPCVAL, and SNGVAL keywords.
DFT	Default	A default value that you assign to the element.
VALUES	Values	This keyword specifies up to 300 values that are valid for the element. Used with RSTD(*YES).

ELEM Statement Keywords, continued

REL	Relationship	This keyword enforces the specified relationship between the PARM and a constant, or between the PARM and another PARM.
RANGE	Range	A range of values that you specify as valid for the element.
SPCVAL	Special values	This keyword lets you specify up to 300 valid values that users can enter for the element. These values do not have to meet the PARM's validity requirements. This keyword can be used to translate an entered value to another value.
MIN	Minimum number of values	A value that defines the minimum number of values that a user can enter. MIN(1) is used to make an element mandatory.
MAX	Maximum number of values	A value that defines the maximum number of values that a user can enter. MAX is used to define a simple list.
FULL	Full entry	A value of *YES forces the number of characters entered for the element to be equal to the length of the element.
CHOICE	Choice text	This keyword specifies the CHOICE text that displays to the right of the input field. There are five options: 1. Up to 30 characters of fixed text. 2. *VALUES, which will display all possible values (based on DFT, SPCVAL, SNGVAL, VALUES, etc.). 3. A message identifier, used to retrieve the CHOICE text. 4. *PGM, to use a choice exit program to retrieve the choice text and permissible values list. 5. *NONE, to display no choice text.
PROMPT	Prompt	This keyword specifies the prompt text, which displays to the left of the input field. Can be up to 30 characters if fixed text or a message identifier used to retrieve the prompt text. The PROMPT keyword can also determine the order in which parameters appear on the prompt screen if you specify an optional relative prompt number.

Summary of
QUAL Statement Keywords

The QUAL statement defines qualified-name parameters, so most of its keywords are identical to those of the PARM statement. This book covers the keywords in this table.

QUAL Statement Keywords		
TYPE	Type	A value that defines the PARM's attributes, such as character, decimal, and so on. (See Appendix B: Parameter Types.)
LEN	Length	This keyword determines the length (and decimal positions, if decimal type) of the PARM.
CONSTANT	Constant	CONSTANT passes a fixed value from the command to the CPP. A PARM with a CONSTANT value is not displayed on the prompt screen. This keyword can be used as a placeholder for dummy parameters. It is also used to create sample command macros without a CPP.
RSTD	Restricted	A value of *YES restricts input to this parameter to the values specified on the VALUES, SPCVAL, and SNGVAL keywords.
DFT	Default	This keyword lets you assign a default value to the PARM.
VALUES	Values	VALUES specifies up to 300 values that are valid for the PARM. Used with RSTD(*YES).

QUAL Statement Keywords, continued		
REL	Relationship	This keyword enforces the specified relationship between the PARM and a constant, or between the PARM and another PARM.
RANGE	Range	RANGE specifies a range of values that are valid for the PARM.
SPCVAL	Special values	SPCVAL specifies up to 300 valid values that the user can enter for the PARM. These values do not have to meet the PARM's validity requirements. This keyword may be used to translate an entered value to another value.
MIN	Minimum number of values	A value that defines the minimum number of vaues that a user can enter. MIN(1) is used to make a PARM mandatory.
FULL	Full entry	A value of *YES forces the number of characters entered for the PARM to be equal to the length of the PARM.
CHOICE	Choice text	This keyword specifies the CHOICE text that displays to the right of the input field. There are five options: 1. Up to 30 characters of fixed text. 2. *VALUES, which will display all possible values (based on DFT, SPCVAL, SNGVAL, VALUES, etc.). 3. A message identifier, used to retrieve the CHOICE text. 4. *PGM, to use a choice exit program to retrieve the choice text and permissible values list. 5. *NONE, to display no choice text.
PROMPT	Prompt	This keyword specifies the prompt text, which displays to the left of the input field. Can be up to 30 characters of fixed text or a message identifier used to retrieve the prompt text. The PROMPT keyword can also determine the order in which parameters appear on the prompt screen if you specify an optional relative prompt number.

Summary of PMTCTL Statement Keywords

Appendix F

The Prompt Control statement defines conditions for presenting parameters for prompting.

PMTCTL Statement Keywords		
CTL	Controlling parameter	This keyword specifies the keyword of the parameter to be tested.
COND	Condition	COND specifies the conditions to be tested (up to 50 conditions).
NBRTRUE	Number true	NBRTRUE specifies the number of conditions that must be true to present the parameter for prompting.
LGLREL	Logical relationship	LGLREL specifies whether the relationship between this PMTCTL statement and the previous one is an AND or an OR relationship.

Summary of
DEP Statement Keywords

Appendix G

The Dependency statement defines required relationships between parameters.

DEP Statement Keywords		
CTL	Controlling conditions	This keyword specifies the conditions under which to test for the dependency.
PARM	Parameter	PARM defines the parameters and relationships to be tested for the dependency.
NBRTRUE	Number true	NBRTRUE defines the number of relationships that must be true for the dependency.
MSGID	Message identifier	MSGID specifies the message ID number to retrieve and display when the dependent relationship is not satisfied.

Index

function of, 104
language, 104
name specification, 104
parameters, 105–106
permissible values list, 106
permissible values with description, 110
RPG warehouse example, 107–108
second parameter structure, 105–106
steps for using, 103
valid entries list, 105
CHOICE keyword
ELEM statement, 144
PARM statement, 13, 17, 140
QUAL statement, 146
CL Programming, 116
*CMD object type, 7
CMD statement, 9–11
PROMPT keyword, 9
prompt screens and, 10
screen heading and, 10
summary, 135
See also Command definition statements
*CNAME parameter type, 137
Command attributes
changeable, list of, 95
changing, 95–97
specifying, 95
See also CHGCMD (Change Command) command
Command defaults
changing, 97–99
changing examples, 98–99
See also CHGCMDDFT (Change Command
Default) command
Command definition statements, 7
CMD, 9–11
DEP, 57–61
ELEM, 26–28
keywords, 8
PARM, 10, 13–22
PMTCTL, 50–55
QUAL, 41–45
summary of, 135
Command processing program (CPP), 7–8
changing with CHGCMD, 96
command creation without, 86–87
for compound list, 36
CONSTANT keyword passing name to, 85
for CRTCMD, 9
for DUPSPLF, 44–45
list processing in, 32

for many commands, 82–85
for mixed list, 33
naming, 8
parameters passed to, 21
QCMDEXC as, 87
for simple list, 34
Command source members
compiling, 8
statements, 7
Commands
with additional parameters function, 49
creation overview, 7–11
custom, 3
defined, 1
IBM-supplied, 2
for macro-like functions, 2
message file uses in, 65
one CPP for many, 82–85
for selective prompting, 2–3
showing additional parameters, 49
for user prompting, 2
user-defined, 1–2
uses for, 2–3
See also Prompt screens; *specific
commands*
Compound lists, 29–32
application example of, 31
CPP for, 36
creating, 31–32
custom example, 31
defined, 29
illustrated, 30
number of, 36, 37
offset of, 36, 37
parameter examples, 37, 38
passing in reverse, 38
processing, 36–40
structure of, 37
uses for, 29
See also Lists
COND keyword, PMTCTL statement, 54, 147
Conditional prompting, 47–55
additional parameters, 47–50
conditioning other parameters, 50–55
defined, 47
types of, 47
See also Prompting
Conditioning other parameters, 50–55
application example, 52–53
defined, 50

RSTD keyword, 143
SPCVAL keyword, 79, 144
summary, 135
TYPE keyword, 143
VALUES keyword, 143
See also Command definition statements
*END special value, 77–78
English message file, 69
Error messages, 113–114
  creating, 114–116
  prompt screen with, 114
  See also Message files

F
F10 (additional parameters), 47–48
FNDSBM command
  with conditional prompting, 52
  displaying conditioned parameters, 53
  source member, 53–54
French message file, 70
FULL keyword
  ELEM statement, 144
  PARM statement, 140
  QUAL statement, 146

G
*GENERIC parameter type, 137
German message file, 70

H
Help. *See* Online help
Help key, 129–130
Help panel groups, 8, 127
  beginning of, 129
  boundaries, 129
  source member, 128–130
  See also User Interface Manager (UIM)
*HEX parameter type, 137
High-level language (HLL) programs
  calling, 2, 7
  QCMDEXC in, 86

I
IBM-supplied commands, 2
  CHGCMD with, 96–97
  See also Commands; Custom commands
*INT2 parameter type, 137
*INT4 parameter type, 137

K
Key parameters, 121, 123
  number of, 123

size of, 123
KEYPARM keyword, 121, 122
  function of, 122
  PARM statement, 141
  specifying, 121
Keyword list
  CHOICE, 13, 17, 140, 144
  COND, 54, 147
  CONSTANT, 82–87, 139, 143
  CTL, 54, 59, 60, 147, 149
  DFT, 13, 16, 139, 143, 145
  FULL, 140, 144, 146
  KEYPARM, 121, 122, 141
  KWD, 13, 14–15, 139
  LEN, 13, 15, 139, 143, 145
  LGLREL, 55, 147
  MAX, 26, 34, 140, 144
  MIN, 13, 16, 140, 144, 146
  MSGID, 61, 149
  NBRTRUE, 55, 59, 147, 149
  PARM, 59, 149
  PMTCTL, 47, 48, 50, 53, 54, 140
  PROMPT, 9, 13, 15–16, 65, 141, 144, 146
  RANGE, 13, 16–17, 140, 144, 146
  REL, 13, 20, 140, 144, 146
  REST, 43
  RSTD, 26, 139, 145
  SPCVAL, 77–82, 140, 144, 146
  TYPE, 13, 15, 19–20, 139, 143, 145
  VALUES, 13, 26, 140, 143, 145
Keywords
  checking for values in, 60
  command definition statement, 8
  DEP statement, 58–59, 149
  ELEM statement, 143–144
  PARM statement, 13, 14–17, 77–87,
    139–141
  PMTCTL statement, 54–55, 147
  QUAL statement, 43–44, 145–146
  See also Keyword list
KWD keyword, PARM statement, 13, 14–15, 139

L
Languages
  libraries for, 69
  message file support, 69–72
LEN keyword
  ELEM statement, 143
  PARM statement, 13, 15, 139
    QUAL statement, 145

example with, 86–87
in HLL programs, 86
parameters passed to, 86, 87
selective prompting with, 93–94
uses, 86
using as CPP, 87
QDATSEP system value, 20
QPNLSRC, 128
QUAL statement, 41–45
CHOICE keyword, 146
coding, 42–44
CONSTANT keyword, 145
default values, changing, 97
DFT keyword, 145
FULL keyword, 146
keywords, 43–44, 145–146
LEN keyword, 145
MIN keyword, 146
PROMPT keyword, 146
RANGE keyword, 146
REL keyword, 146
RSTD keyword, 145
SPCVAL keyword, 146
summary, 135
TYPE keyword, 44, 145
using, 43
VALUES keyword, 145
See also Command definition statements
Qualified fields
coding, 43
defining, 42–43
PARMs vs., 44
Qualified parameters, 41–45
illustrated, 41
layout, 45
processing, 44–45
uses for, 42
See also Parameters
Question mark (?), 89, 91

R
RANGE keyword
ELEM statement, 144
PARM statement, 13, 16–17, 140
QUAL statement, 146
REL keyword
ELEM statement, 144
PARM statement, 13, 20, 140
QUAL statement, 146
Relationships
defining, 59–60

definition limit, 59
dependent, 57–61
RSTD keyword, 26
ELEM statement, 143
PARM statement, 139
QUAL statement, 145
RSTOBJ (Restore Object) command, 23
OBJ parameter, 24
prompt screen, 24
RUNQRY (Run Query) command, 93, 94
CHGCMD command on, 96–97
preventing interactive running, 96

S
SBMJOB (Submit Job) command, 52
Job name parameter, 92
OUTQ parameter, 93
prompt screen, 93
selective prompting with, 92–93
Selective prompting, 2–3, 89–94
() in value specification, 91
?special characters, 92
?& special characters, 92
?* special characters, 90, 92
?< special characters, 92
?- special characters, 90, 92
?? special characters, 90, 92
?/ special characters, 92
characters, 89–91, 92
defined, 89
for dynamic defaults, 93
options, 91–92
with QCMDEXC API, 93–94
with SBMJOB command, 92–93
value specification method, 91
WRKUSRJOB command form, 90
See also Prompting
SEU, using, 7–8
Simple lists, 23–26
CL program for processing, 35
CPP for, 34
defined, 23
illustrated, 24
passing, 34
processing, 34–36
specifying, 26
uses, 24–25
See also Lists
*SNAME parameter type, 137
SPCVAL keyword, 77–82
for abbreviating values, 80–82